For Betsy —
great old friend

Letters to Alice

NUMBER TWENTY-TWO:
Gulf Coast Books
Sponsored by Texas A&M University–Corpus Christi
John W. Tunnell Jr., *General Editor*

Frances B. Vick
Jane Clements Monday

A list of all titles in this series
is available at the end of the book.

An artist's rendering of Robert and Alice Kleberg from a photograph thought to have been taken at the time of their wedding on June 17, 1886. Illustration by Barbara Mathews Whitehead.

Letters to Alice

Birth of the Kleberg-King Ranch Dynasty

EDITED AND ANNOTATED BY

Jane Clements Monday *and* Frances Brannen Vick

With a Foreword by

Thomas H. Kreneck

Texas A&M University Press

College Station

FIRST EDITION

This paper meets the requirements of ANSI/NISO Z39.48-1992
(Permanence of Paper).
Binding materials have been chosen for durability.

The front jacket illustration and frontispiece are from Barbara Mathews Whitehead's rendering of Robert and Alice Kleberg from a photograph thought to have been taken at the time of their wedding on June 17, 1886.
Courtesy Barbara Mathews Whitehead.

Library of Congress Cataloging-in-Publication Data
Kleberg, Robert Justus, 1853–1932.
Letters to Alice : birth of the Kleberg-King Ranch dynasty / edited and annotated by Jane Clements Monday and Frances Brannen Vick ; with a foreword by Thomas H. Kreneck. — 1st ed.
p. cm. — (Gulf Coast books ; no. 22)
Includes bibliographical references and index.
ISBN-13: 978-1-60344-471-2 (cloth : alk. paper)
ISBN-10: 1-60344-471-8 (cloth : alk. paper)
ISBN-13: 978-1-60344-331-9 (e-book)
ISBN-10: 1-60344-331-2 (e-book)
1. Kleberg, Robert Justus, 1853–1932—Correspondence. 2. Kleberg, Alice Gertrudis King, 1862–1944—Correspondence. 3. Kleberg, Robert Justus, 1853–1932. 4. Kleberg, Alice Gertrudis King, 1862–1944. 5. Ranchers—Texas—Biography. 6. Lawyers—Texas—Biography. 7. Ranchers' spouses—Texas—Biography. 8. King Ranch (Tex.)—History. I. Monday, Jane Clements, 1941– II. Vick, Frances Brannen, 1935– III. Kleberg, Alice Gertrudis King, 1862–1944. IV. Title. V. Series: Gulf Coast books ; no. 22.
F391.K63A4 2012
976.4'113—dc23   2011047715

To my family, whose support is outstanding: my wonderful husband Charles, our children and their spouses Kimberly, Lauren, Julie, Buddie, Jennifer, and Adam, and our grandchildren Jack, Ellie, Sarah, Ben, Sam, Annie, Caroline, and Charlie. I give you all my deepest love and appreciation. To our Leadership Texas Class of 1990, who have become our sisters and supporters through the years: I join with Fran in our appreciation of the true meaning of friendship.

—Jane Monday

To the women who made all the difference in my life: Bess, who was first, then Marilyn, and the ones who came later—Ellen, Jane, Mary Etta, Gayla, Joyce, Laura, Judy, Liz, Phyllis, Sharon, Jane M., Diane, Carla, Jerry, and the Leadership Texas Class of 1990.

—Fran Vick

Contents

Foreword

THE SPECIAL COLLECTIONS & Archives Department of the Mary and Jeff Bell Library, Texas A&M University–Corpus Christi, is gratified to be involved in publishing these edited letters from Robert Justus Kleberg Sr. (1853–1932) to Alice Gertrudis King (1862–1944), prominent figures in the establishment of King Ranch. Jane Clements Monday and Frances Brannen Vick have fashioned this correspondence into a significant volume on the history of South Texas. It contributes to the literature on King Ranch and illuminates the life and times of not only the young man who wrote the letters and the young woman who received them during courtship and early marriage but also the people and events of the Victorian-era world in which they lived.

Although authors/editors Monday and Vick elaborate at length on the correspondence, let me introduce several dimensions of special importance. First, the letters supplement our knowledge of King Ranch, which many scholars see as a paradigm of Texas and US ranching. In particular, they shed light on the union between Robert and Alice, members of the Kleberg and King families that marked a new and important departure in the development of that ranching enterprise. The correspondence reveals how their courtship involved Alice's parents, the legendary Captain Richard King and Henrietta Chamberlain King. The letters thus show a less well known but profoundly human side of these early figures of the most celebrated ranching family in South Texas.

The Klebergs and Kings were significant not only in the history of ranching but also in Corpus Christi urban development. They saw Corpus Christi as a seasonal residence and as an important outlet to the sea for the agricultural goods of the hinterlands, of which King Ranch formed a part. Robert Kleberg Sr. came to Corpus Christi in the early 1880s to practice law in the fledgling town and stayed in the region for the rest of his life. His comments offer glimpses into the legal profession as well as the web of social and business networks within which these families dwelled. Kleberg also provides insights into the life of a working Corpus Christi and Texas attorney as he shares his activities with his bride-to-be. On occasion, he also shares his political observations with her.

The book gives the reader an intimate look at courtship during this era. The Kleberg-King letters shed light on interpersonal relationships and patterns of courting in the late nineteenth century, when letter writing allowed people to express their feelings in an indelible manner. The correspondence reflects the sentiments of a love-struck (and somewhat possessive) gentleman for the object of his affections. He is a fellow smitten, a man thoroughly human and attentive to his future wife's feelings. Only the most barren soul could not savor the genteel but intense love story that is told in his letters.

As with all publications, several people played key roles in this production. Most importantly, Jane Clements Monday and Frances Brannen Vick were the precise scholars to deal with this material. Their work on the Kenedy-King relationship in their monumental *Petra's Legacy: The South Texas Ranching Empire of Petra Vela and Mifflin Kenedy* (2007) qualified them as such. Their ongoing association with the Special Collections & Archives Department likewise placed them in good stead. Monday and Vick should be commended for the meticulous job they have done with this correspondence. Amply footnoted and annotated, their work represents solid analytical history; happily for us, they have also provided a readable narrative.

Other people close to this publication include the late Robert E. Skabelund, who acquired these letters during the 1940s while in the armed services in Corpus Christi and subsequently donated the letters to Special Collections & Archives. Because of Mr. Skabelund, they are now part of the department's permanent holdings. Only through the foresight and generosity of such donors can historical treasures like these be saved and made available for scholarship. The department also wishes to express its appreciation to Rick Stryker and Donald P. Zuris of the Corpus Christi Museum of Science and History for referring the donor to us. Special thanks also go to Jorge D. Canales and Warren J. DeLuca of the Texas A&M University System's Office of General Counsel for their crucial legal assistance in this project.

Bruce S. Cheeseman, former archivist and historian for King Ranch, researcher extraordinaire, and my personal friend, likewise did much to foster this book. A wealth of information on King Ranch and South Texas history, Bruce proved particularly valuable in verifying the handwriting of Robert J. Kleberg Sr. and in deciphering many of the illegible words in his letters. Bruce's many years of working with the nineteenth-century script of King Ranch people have given him added sensitivity and appreciation for their contributions to the area. Cecilia G. Venable, staff member of Special Collections & Archives, provided a great deal of research assistance, image duplication, and other services necessary to produce this volume.

Curators of manuscripts, rare books, and other historical documents have an obligation not only to preserve the items under their care but also to foster their open use to edify the public. This imperative to disseminate knowledge especially holds true for a repository within an institution of higher learning. Such a commitment prompted the editing and publication of these letters. The Special Collections & Archives Department thus envisions this worthy volume as another step in its own mission to promote the study of the South Texas past.

Thomas H. Kreneck
Associate Director for Special Collections & Archives
Joe B. Frantz Lecturer in Public History
Texas A&M University-Corpus Christi

Preface

When Thomas H. Kreneck, head of Special Collections & Archives at Bell Library, Texas A&M University–Corpus Christi, called us about editing a small cache of love letters from Robert Kleberg to Alice King, we jumped at the chance. It seemed the perfect follow-up to our work on *Petra's Legacy: The South Texas Ranching Empire of Petra Vela and Mifflin Kenedy.* We already knew about Alice's parents, Richard and Henrietta King, because of their closeness to Petra and Mifflin Kenedy, and had immersed ourselves in the details of their lives during the research and writing of *Petra's Legacy.* Alice King and Robert Kleberg would be the next generation in that South Texas saga of the taming of the Wild Horse Desert. What we did not know before we started doing research for this book was the depth of the love Robert Kleberg had for his "Little Heart," Alice King, as shown in the letters he wrote to her and that we have edited for publication here. These are truly Victorian love letters. They show a deepening love between these two people, the traumas they went through, and their emergence as a couple ready and able to carry on the legacy and ensure the dynasty that Richard and Henrietta had begun.

The first job was to transcribe the letters. Robert Kleberg's handwriting would fit the old stereotype of a medical doctor's indecipherable penmanship. As a result, there may be some errors in the transcriptions, and we simply could not decipher some words and names at all; we have indicated doubt with a question mark within brackets [?]. Some words are missing because of physical damage to the letters, and we indicate those with another bracketed notation: [torn and illegible]. Perhaps someone reading this book will recognize some of the names that were in doubt and contact the publisher. When a letter had an envelope, the transcription begins with the text Robert wrote on the envelope; editorial explanations of his address text are in brackets.

Robert Kleberg wrote these letters from the top of each sheet of paper to the bottom, and then he would turn the page on its side and write in both margins. He was being thrifty in his efficient use of paper, but he made it incredibly difficult to transcribe the letters; one wonders how Alice could read them. Among Robert's other epistolary offenses were his regular use of dashes rather than periods, his sometimes faulty spelling, and his failure to use paragraph breaks. Many letters were essentially one long sentence. We took the liberty of inserting paragraph breaks and using punctuation where it seemed necessary to make sense of what Robert was writing. If we misinterpreted Robert's intentions, we apologize to all.

Because several generations of Klebergs bore the same names, we have employed the following pattern (unless otherwise indicated) to identify the specific Robert Kleberg being discussed: **Robert Justus Kleberg I** is the father of the letter writer, **Robert Justus Kleberg Sr.** is the letter writer, and **Robert Justus Kleberg Jr.** is the son of the letter writer. References simply to "Robert" indicate the letter writer (unless otherwise noted).

We decided that the most reader-friendly way to indicate to what or whom Robert was referring would be to insert explanations directly into the letters in a different typeface rather than putting all explanations in the endnotes. Our fervent hope is that the editorial voice does not intrude too much into the letters, for they are the priceless writings of a Victorian-era man who is courting and pursuing the woman he intends to marry.

To help acquaint the reader with Robert and Alice and their respective families, we offer some context at the beginning and end of each letter. When there were chronological gaps between the letters, we included transitions to apprise the reader of what was occurring in the couple's lives during that time. We have been surprised to discover that there is little published information about either Robert Kleberg Sr. or Alice King, despite the fact that they kept the King Ranch dynasty alive to pass on to future generations.

We hope that readers become as fascinated with the intrigues surrounding these two lovers as we did and as the South Texas community must have been when the couple's courtship was in progress; the Corpus Christi gossip must have been fast and furious! After all, Alice was Captain Richard King's "princess," and Robert was one of the most eligible bachelors in South Texas. In addition to political intrigue and the dynamics of the two families—the Kings and the Klebergs—we discovered much about Robert and Alice and the world in which they moved.

To complete this project, we divided up the work. Fran Vick primarily transcribed and annotated the letters, while Jane Monday wrote the opening and concluding chapters and the transitions. Of course we also shared our texts with each other as we progressed and thus got each other's input along the way.

We had tremendous help at every step. At the Special Collections & Archives Department of the Mary and Jeff Bell Library, Texas A&M University–Corpus Christi, Tom Kreneck, who has done much work on South Texas, and Cecilia G. Venable were our guides. Bruce Cheeseman, former archivist at the King Ranch, was familiar with Robert Kleberg's handwriting and helped with the transcription. Richard Leshin was very helpful with his information on the Kleberg law firm, and once again Homero Vera stepped into the breach to help us. We are grateful to Barbara Whitehead for her drawing of Alice and Robert, to Tara Carlisle for her cheerful help with photographs from the University of North Texas Libraries, and to David Gracy for his always helpful suggestions for possible photographs. We also thank Denise Tillson at the Huntsville Public Library and Cheryl Spencer from the Thomason Room at the Sam Houston State University Library for all of their help. We thank Allison Ehrlich of the *Corpus Christi Caller-Times;* Linda Briscoe Myers and Roy L. Flukinger of the Photographic Collection at the Harry Ransom Center at the University of Texas at Austin; Nancy Sparrow, curatorial assistant at the Alexander Architectural Archive, Architecture and Planning Library, University of Texas Libraries, University of Texas at Austin; and Aryn Glazier, photography services coordinator, Dolph Briscoe Center for American History, University of Texas at Austin. And we thank Anne Peterson, Cynthia Franco, and Russell Martin of the DeGolyer Library at Southern Methodist University for their always courteous and expedient help. Our heartfelt thanks go to copyeditor Maureen Creamer Bemko for her outstanding work.

We also want to thank our incredibly supportive families: Charles Monday, Kim Monday, Lauren Marangell, Julie and Buddie Ballard, Jennifer and Adam Goldman, and grandchildren Sarah, Ben, Sam, Annie, Caroline, Charlie, Jack, and Ellie for Jane. For Fran: children Karen and Sam Cavazos, Ross and Julie Vick, Patrick and Nelda Vick; grandchildren Courtney and Pete Neria and their children, Ashleigh, Seth, and Nathan; Kathy and Ryan Stopani and their children Emily and Christopher; Taylor, Brannen, and Ginna Vick, especially for Ginna's help with transcribing the letters; and Ross IV and Jessica and their daughter Ella Bel. All of them are there for us, always. Finally, we thank our good friends at Texas A&M University Press: Editor-in-Chief Mary Lenn Dixon, Managing Editor Thom Lemmons, Marketing Manager Gayla Christiansen and her delightful team of Caitlin Churchill, Holli Estridge, and Kyle Littlefield, and Mary Ann Jacob, the press's award-winning design manager. None of this would be possible without all of you.

Letters to Alice

This photograph of Robert J. Kleberg Sr. (1853–1932) was taken circa 1878 in Austin, Texas, by photographer Hamilton Biscoe Hillyer. Robert would have been about twenty-five years old at the time the photograph was taken. DeGolyer Library, Central University Libraries, Southern Methodist University.

Prologue, 1853–1883

On July 24, 1881, twenty-seven-year-old Robert Justus Kleberg sat down at his desk to write to his parents about a recent trip he had taken, one that would ultimately change his life. Robert was just beginning his law career. He had attended the law course at the University of Virginia the year before, been admitted to the bar in Texas, and started a practice in Cuero before moving to Corpus Christi, where he formed a law partnership with Judge John W. Stayton.[1]

A Desert Empire

Robert entered the legal profession on the heels of his father; law had thus come naturally for Robert. Robert Justus Kleberg I, a respected lawyer, also served as chief justice of DeWitt County.[2] He and his wife, Philippine Sophie Caroline Luise Rosalie von Roeder (usually known as Rosalie or Rosa), and their extended family had come to Texas from Prussia in 1834. The von Roeders had a familial connection to the Prussian nobleman Simon Heinrich Sack, who had arranged to provide scholarships to male family members and dowries for female members; this provided the von Roeder/Kleberg clans a unique opportunity on the Texas frontier. Robert used his legacy to pay for his law training in Virginia.[3]

The Kleberg family had distinguished itself almost immediately upon arriving in Texas. The Prussian immigrant, Robert Kleberg I,

Robert Justus Kleberg I (1803–1888), a Prussian immigrant with urbane manners and courtly style, became a well-known lawyer in early Texas. Rare Book and Texana Collections, University of North Texas Libraries.

Rosalie von Roeder, the mother of Robert J. Kleberg Sr., was an accomplished musician and is credited with bringing the first piano to Texas. Rare Book and Texana Collections, University of North Texas Libraries.

fought at San Jacinto and helped to guard the captured Santa Anna. General Sam Houston then appointed Kleberg to be a judge on the land commission.[4]

Rosalie was an accomplished musician and is credited with bringing the first piano to Texas, in the spring of 1835. When she and part of the family fled during the Runaway Scrape, they had to leave their possessions behind. When Kickapoo Indians burned their house, the piano burned with it.[5]

The Klebergs moved to DeWitt County, first to Cat Spring in 1847 and then to Meyersville, where they raised their children. There was no school when they arrived in DeWitt County, so Judge Kleberg and other settlers erected a log cabin alongside Coleto Creek and thus established education in the area.[6]

Rosalie and Robert Kleberg had three sons and four daughters. Being a believer in states' rights and local self-government as well as a learned man who knew Greek, Latin, and three modern languages, Robert Kleberg I expected much of his children, especially his sons, and they did not disappoint him.[7] Rudolph, born in 1847, graduated from college, taught school at Yorktown, studied law in San Antonio, was admitted to the bar, and began his practice in Cuero. While there, he established the *Cuero Star* and was editor for four years. He also served as county attorney for DeWitt County and in 1882 was elected to the Texas Senate. In 1885, President Grover Cleveland appointed him US attorney for the Western District of Texas, a position he held until 1889. In April 1896, he was elected to fill the vacancy in the US Congress left by the death of his law partner, and he served until 1903.[8] The next son, Marcellus, was born in 1849. He graduated from the law school of Washington and Lee University and established his law practice in DeWitt County. He served in the Thirteenth Texas Legislature and later moved his law practice to Galveston, where he served as city attorney, city commissioner, and as a trustee and president of the school board. He was a regent of the University of Texas under Governor S. W. T. Lanham.[9]

The sons of Robert Justus Kleberg I and Rosalie von Roeder were Marcellus (left), who served in the legislature, was a city official in Galveston, and a University of Texas regent; Robert (seated); and Rudolph (right), who served in the Texas state senate, was US attorney for the Western District of Texas, and served in the US Congress from 1896 to 1903. Rare Book and Texana Collections, University of North Texas Libraries.

The farmhouse where Robert and Rosalie Kleberg made their home was located near Cat Spring, Texas, which got its name when Louis von Roeder, Rosalie's brother, killed a wildcat nearby. An architecture study of the house in 1957 indicated it had originally been a three-room house with a second story; another room and an indoor stairway were added later. The farmstead included an outside kitchen and smokehouse, outhouse, hog pen, hay barn, cow pen, cotton house, calf pen, garden, water well, and planting areas for cotton and sweet potatoes. Texas Architecture Archive Collection, Alexander Architectural Archive, Architecture and Planning Library, University of Texas Libraries, University of Texas at Austin.

The youngest son, Robert, born in 1853, attended Concrete Academy, located on the banks of the Guadalupe River. It charged one hundred dollars for five months of schooling and two hundred for ten months, a sum that was hard to come by for the farmers in the community. Concrete Academy stressed education in the classics and business. Courses in penmanship, music, and foreign and classical languages were offered as well. The academy was very strict when it came to pupils who indulged in games of chance, smoking, profane language, and the use of liquor, which was cause for expulsion.[10] The school day started early, with mandatory chapel attendance at 5:10 a.m. Chapel lasted until 6:30 a.m., when the first classes of the day began. Students did not eat breakfast until 9:00 a.m., and they spent the remainder of the day in class, studying, or working around the academy. A two-hour study period, between 7:00 and 9:00 p.m. ended the day.[11]

Thus, when young Robert sought to establish himself in Corpus Christi as a lawyer, he did so with a solid family reputation and relatives who were influential throughout the state. Judge Kleberg was well known, as were Robert's two older brothers. Little did he know that when he started out on his trip that he would be visiting frontier royalty and meeting his future wife and love of his life.

In the summer of 1881, as a new lawyer in Corpus Christi, Robert was in court facing two formidable Texans: Captains Richard King and Mifflin Kenedy. The two men had come to Texas during the US-Mexican War in 1846 to operate boats on the Rio Grande for the US Army. The two men had stayed in Texas after the war to make their fortunes and had succeeded. They started out by establishing a monopoly in the steamboat business following the war and then maintaining lucrative government contracts. When the Civil War began, they created a network to buy Confederate cotton using Confederate dollars, then smuggled the cotton to Mexico, and finally sold it to buyers from Europe and the northeastern United States who paid them with gold coins. With their profits, they left Brownsville in 1869 and invested in large ranches in the middle of the Wild Horse Desert of South Texas, thus establishing cattle empires.

Captain Richard King respected talented lawyers and had always employed the best he could find in Texas. His entire empire rested on their ability to secure land titles that were free and clear and sanctioned by the courts. When the young Robert Kleberg bested him in the courts in the summer of 1881, he took immediate notice and invited him to visit his home at Rancho Santa Gertrudis. Robert accepted the invitation, and it was that trip to King's ranch about which he wrote to his mother and father on July 24, 1881:

Captain King had written to come out to see him and to name the day and he would meet me at the road as he lives about eighteen mile from the railroad so I went on the railroad and found him waiting for me at the depot with his carriage. He runs a regular wagon to the depot daily to bring in his mail and supplies but it had no seats. He said his carriage would be there if I notified him. We had a delightful trip out to his ranch—he drove a pair of fine fast horses and in two hours we were at his ranch. He had plenty of ice, wine, and cigars so the heat did not bother us much. At the ranch a table was loaded with good things to eat and drink; he lives like a prince and has a regular French cook. He treats his friends to the best he has. I stayed at his house from Monday until Saturday morning. We rode all day and he showed me his land. He has 1,000,000 acres of land. Near the lakes where the cattle come to drink could be seen as many as 3,000 head at a time. On Saturday morning he sent me back to the R.R. depot and furnished [me] with suitable wine and ice on the way. He wants us to attend his business for him and I hope we are to find it remunerative.[12]

When Robert traveled to the ranch by train from Corpus Christi, he passed through the beginning of the Wild Horse Desert, which stretches from Corpus Christi and the Nueces River south across the vast, uninhabited landscape to the Rio Grande and the border with Mexico. When there was rain, as there often was in the springtime, the sand hills were covered with waving grass, wildflowers, and live oaks and grapevines. The wind blew constantly across the rolling hills, bringing with it the scent of the sea from the nearby coast. The thickets of mesquite and cacti, including prickly pears, bloomed profusely, filling the landscape with bright yellow and purple flowers. By July, though, the flowers were gone, and the dust and heat reminded everyone that they were in the middle of a desert.[13] It was this wild land that prompted Union general Philip Sheridan to comment that if he "owned both places he would rent Texas and live in hell."[14]

After arriving at Collins Station in the ranch country and climbing aboard Captain King's carriage, Robert must have stolen some looks at

Captain Richard King established his Rancho Santa Gertrudis in 1853. Robert Kleberg stated that when he first saw the ranch, in 1881, it encompassed more than a half million acres. Brownsville Historical Association, Brownsville, Texas.

the legendary rancher. The captain was "a striking figure with a wide-brimmed black hat, black string tie, dark broadcloth coat, rumpled pants, and always scuffed boots. His black beard reached the second button on his shirt. Captain King had a slight limp caused either by an injury when his leg was broken by moving an anchor chain on a steamboat or, as the vaqueros claimed, from a snake bite. His vaqueros called him El Cojo, the lame one. He also had a disfigured left nostril that was caused when his wife's parrot bit him on the nose."[15]

Captain King may have been scarred by adversity, but he triumphed over it and continued to present an impressive countenance. "Steel gray eyes, a slow deliberate speech, a mouth as stern as Caesar, and a smile like the gleam of the blue pole-star on the lonely Arctic seas, he never hurried, but his eagle eye, retentive brain and lynx-like ear never missed any activity" was one early writer's description of him.[16] With that “eagle eye,” he could spot a moving form on the desert and identify it faster than a person using a spyglass. Despite having no familiarity with books, he had the whole map of Texas in his mind, and he always had the ablest advisers he could find gathered around him. He was often rude and wholly wrapped up in his business schemes but was devoted to the modest woman who had given him the children of his heart.[17]

Richard King once testified that he was born in New York City on July 10, 1824. He said that his parents apprenticed him to a jeweler when he was nine because they were so poor, but at the age of eleven he ran off and stowed away on the sailing ship *Desdemona*. The ship's captain discovered him but allowed the boy to stay. He later went to work as a “cub” for Joe Holland, a steamboat captain who made the run from Mobile to Montgomery on the Alabama River. The Holland family took an interest in the unlettered cub and taught the boy to read and figure. They later sent Richard to live with other members of the Holland family, and he attended school for eight months, which was the only formal education he ever had.[18] Despite King's testimony as to his birthplace, the 1860 and 1870 Texas census records list Richard King as born in Ireland and his children are listed as having a foreign-born father.[19] Whether King was born in Ireland or New York, by 1881 he had become one of the most powerful men in Texas and certainly one of the wealthiest.

As the captain and Robert Kleberg rode the eighteen miles to Rancho Santa Gertrudis with the wind whipping in their faces, the young lawyer got his first glance at the land that would some day be his home and a legacy to his descendants. When Captain King had established his cow camp twenty-eight years before, in 1853, there had been almost no permanent inhabitants in the area. He had put down his roots on the banks of the Santa Gertrudis Creek and vowed to stay. The rancho that Robert saw consisted of more than half a million acres.[20] As has been observed, “The land was like a feudal state maintained by force of arms, galloping horses and imperious wills.”[21]

Captain King's ranch hands, known as the Kineños, were like

armed soldiers that had to camp under the stars through heat and drought or flooding rains and cold northers to maintain the vast acreage. One of Captain King's granddaughters later said that if she was sent to milk a cow on the upper pasture, she would have to take along a camp outfit, a week's grub, and a couple of packhorses.[22]

As they approached the Rancho Santa Gertrudis headquarters, Robert saw on a plateau fifty feet above the plain a huge masonry castle keep that was three stories high; the square tower served as the fortress and look-out post for the ranch. It was like a great princely estate, with two hundred men riding the land to protect it and take care of the owner's possessions. At some little distance from the fortress was a large, Southern-style planter's home that rose from the carefully tended gardens. Beyond the house were extensive office buildings and immense stacks of prairie hay.[23] An open-air walkway connected the house to a detached stone kitchen and dining room that also contained eating and sleeping quarters for extra ranch hands. There was also a row of small houses for the Kineños and their families and a one-room school for the ranch children.[24]

Unpretentious on the outside, the house's interior offered refined luxury. When Robert entered the house, he passed through the great hall, where a forest of mounted trophies represented the game of the ranch. There were robes and skins covering the polished floor and heads of "Big Horn" elk, deer antlers, antelope horns, great bison heads, and open-jawed trophies of bear, panther, jaguar, wolf, and wildcat on every wall. There were eight guest chambers upstairs, and a boy was assigned to serve him while he was there.[25]

Robert and Captain King were probably greeted at the house by the captain's wife, Henrietta Chamberlain King. Henrietta, or "Etta" as the captain called her, was slight of build, soft-spoken, intensely religious, and shy, always shunning the public eye.[26] She was known throughout the land for her hospitality. The daughter of a Presbyterian minister who had come to the Rio Grande Valley to "Christianize" so-called heathens and Catholics, she had been brought up to always do her duty. Her mother died in 1835, when Etta was three years old. Her

In 1857, Captain Richard King built this ranch house on a hill between the Santa Gertrudis and San Fernando creeks, presumably on a site picked by King's friend, Robert E. Lee. This low, rambling structure with a porch gallery was the King home that Robert referred to in his letters to Alice. As the Kleberg family expanded they continued to add on to the home by adding first a second story and then adding to the rear of the house. Unfortunately, the house burned down on January 14, 1912, consuming most of their personal possessions. Corpus Christi Caller-Times, Corpus Christi, Texas.

father married twice more and had eight more children. Henrietta moved from place to place with him, serving as a surrogate mother to her younger siblings. In 1846, when she was fourteen years old, her father sent her to Holly Springs Female Institute in Mississippi, where "planters' daughters received education in grammar, algebra, moral philosophy, and French and domestic uses, ornamental needlework in floss, chenille, worsted beads and gold and silver embroidery."[27] When she was very homesick, her father urged her to be a good "soldier" and have "noble resolution." She finished school in 1848 at age sixteen, and by eighteen she was moving to Brownsville, Texas.[28]

In February 1850, Richard King, then a tired and harassed young steamboat pilot, returned to Brownsville to find the slip for his boat,

Henrietta Chamberlain, the daughter of a Presbyterian clergyman, met riverboat captain Richard King in Brownsville, Texas, in 1850, when she was eighteen and engaged to another man. After her marriage to King in 1854, she devoted her life to the captain, her family, and fulfilling his dream for the King Ranch. Christus Spohn Health Systems, Corpus Christi, Texas.

the *Colonel Cross,* occupied by an old houseboat named the *Whiteville.* He began to express his frustration with "river language" until he saw, with some trepidation, that a dainty young woman had appeared on the deck. She flashed her eyes at him, promptly put him in his place, and left him smitten. Richard went to his friend, Mifflin Kenedy, to find out who the beautiful young lady might be and found that she was the daughter of the new preacher in town, Reverend Hiram Chamberlain. Mifflin had met them already and offered to introduce Richard to Henrietta. He did so one day when they happened to meet on the sidewalk. Henrietta sang in the choir at the newly formed First Presbyterian Church, and Richard often found himself there for Wednesday evening services.[29]

The courtship lasted four years, with Richard exerting a great deal of energy to win the approval of not only Henrietta but also her father. When Henrietta met Richard King, she was engaged to R. N. Stansbury, a serious young man employed as the superintendent of the Sunday school, which had sixteen teachers and seventy-two scholars. Stansbury was, according to a local correspondent, "constantly mourning over what he deems his unfaithfulness to his Christian duties."[30] In May 1851, a year after meeting Richard King, Henrietta broke her engagement to Stansbury.[31] One wonders if Reverend Chamberlain had misgivings about Henrietta rejecting the advances of this young man in favor of a rough, poorly educated, hard-drinking, good-looking Irish steamboat captain. Richard continued his lengthy courtship and finally prevailed three years later.

Henrietta Chamberlain and Richard King married in Brownsville on December 10, 1854, after a church service presided over by her father.[32] One of her granddaughters said of her: "Grandmother seemed bound by the admonitions given to her by her father. The Bible, which she received on the occasion of her marriage, bore the inscription: Mrs. H. Ch. King, from her father, Read, Believe, Obey, and Live. Brownsville, December 10th, 1854."[33]

Captain King had paid four hundred dollars for one large closed carriage and harness at Corpus Christi to carry the couple on their honeymoon to the Rancho Santa Gertrudis or "Kings Folly," as the bride's friends called it. Armed vaqueros riding steeds with flowing manes escorted the newlyweds on their four-day trip. They settled down at the rancho in an adobe hut so small that Henrietta had to hang her pots and pans outside. With her Bible and its inscription to remind her of her duties, she set about being the excellent wife, mother, protector, and hostess of an empire in the making.[34]

Danger surrounded her at every turn, however, and one day, as she was baking bread in the small *jacal* that served as an outdoor kitchen, she looked up and saw an Indian standing silently by the door. The Indian jumped toward the cradle where Henrietta had put her daughter, Nettie, to catch some breeze by the door and raised his club over the baby's head. With his other hand, he motioned toward the delicious-smelling bread. Henrietta quickly gave all of the bread to him, and he departed without harming either one of them.[35] With danger in the land, the captain taught Henrietta to shoot the pistol and rifle he had given her. She kept her weapons and her Bible close by for the rest of her life.[36]

The Rancho Santa Gertrudis became the seat of hospitality for the South Texas ranch country, and it reminded guests of the baronial halls of England in the sense that the doors were opened to all well-behaved comers. Henrietta was noted for her culture, her capability, and her beauty. She was the wise counselor to her husband, his closest confidant, and, most of all, his trusted friend.[37]

Dinner was a formal affair at the rancho, with everyone staying in the home expected to be dressed properly and to conduct themselves with decorum. When the dinner bell was rung, the guests gathered in the parlor and then processed down a long walkway to the outdoor dining area. Captain King sat at the head of the table, set in a grand style that would have suited nobility. The table was laden with the best food and drink, with most of the food served coming from the rancho's own bounty.[38]

Henrietta spent part of each morning with the cooks, deciding on the day's menus. There was food on the stove twenty-four hours a day so that no ranch guest or employee, coming or going, would be without sustenance. She always made her selections from the large garden and from the ranch's wildlife and livestock, including turkey, sheep, lamb, goat, beef, deer, antelope, and a variety of birds. Some of her guests were known to sit down to a fifteen-course meal consisting entirely of food raised at Santa Gertrudis or hunted on its lands.[39] For a special treat, she sometimes had barrels of oysters brought from Corpus Christi, fattened on cornmeal, and later fried for the enjoyment of her guests.[40]

After dinner the women would gather on the portico, where the men would later join them for music. Meanwhile, the men would repair to a small brick building detached from the main house. The building had heavy iron shutters, a folding iron door, and a gigantic safe against the wall. There were racks containing a dozen Winchester, Spencer, and heavy Springfield rifles, along with several rows of revolvers. The room was indeed a fortress. On the wall there were three well-polished bell-pulls, one each for the house, depot, and corral. Captain King could summon fifty armed men in an instant by using these.[41] He also had bell cords in the house.

Adjoining this veritable fortress was a storehouse that held a year's supply of outfitting for two hundred men. Under the horse sheds, fleet animals were kept ready to ride, and most of the men had their personal "Colt's frontier" pistol and a belt of copper cartridges ready to go at all times. The ranch superintendent, corral master, and accountant presided over wayfarers who entered the ranch's territory. Men driving cattle—both English-speaking cowboys and Spanish-speaking vaqueros—received food and shelter, but in separate buildings from the official guests' quarters. From the fortress, the captain could see for fifty miles with his spyglass and prepare for and defend against any attack.[42]

Princess of the Wild Horse Desert

AT SOME POINT DURING Robert Kleberg's first visit to the Rancho Santa Gertrudis, he met the woman who would be the love of his life: Alice Gertrudis King. During that summer of 1881, she was nineteen years old, with dark hair and brown eyes. She was described as having a sweet, serious face and "silken brown tresses [that] shaded her brow."[43] This "Princess of the Wild Horse Desert" immediately captivated Robert. Alice had been born at Rancho Santa Gertrudis on April 29, 1862, during the Civil War, and she lived there her whole life. As the years passed, she gained increasing responsibility, first caring for her father, then her mother, husband, and children. The only time

Alice King, "Princess of the Wild Horse Desert," met Robert Kleberg when she was nineteen years old and her father had taken note of the young lawyer's skills. Christus Spohn Health System, Corpus Christi, Texas.

she left the rancho for an extended period was for schooling. She grew up with her four siblings: Henrietta Maria (called Nettie), born in 1856; Ella Morse, born April 13, 1858; Richard II, born December 15, 1860; and Robert Lee, known as Lee (named for General Robert E. Lee), born on February 22, 1864.[44] The King girls and boys grew up at the ranch speaking Spanish as well as English and feeling at home on horses and the land. Alice was said to have had a particularly regal, dignified bearing in the saddle.[45] Henrietta King began teaching the children at an early age and also hired tutors, Professor Allen and a Mrs. McGuire from Virginia. Also in residence at the house were Henrietta's half brothers—Hiram Jr., Bland, Willie, and Edwin—who had moved to the ranch when Reverend Chamberlain died in 1866. Bland was the only one to stay at the ranch all his life. To provide bedrooms for all the children, the Kings remodeled the main living quarters and added a second story to the house.[46]

The King boys were sent off to school at age fifteen, both going to Centre Presbyterian College in Danville, Kentucky. While there, Richard had his own carriage and manservant.[47] The girls were sent east to school as well, with Nettie enrolling at Henderson Female Institute, a Presbyterian girls' school, also located in Danville, Kentucky, in 1870. The next year Ella and Alice joined her, and by 1875 the girls were back at the ranch.[48]

Captain Leander H. McNelly and his company of Texas Rangers were recipients of Henrietta and her daughters' hospitality when the rangers returned from an extremely dangerous raid into Mexico to recapture stolen Texas cattle. When the men arrived at the ranch, Captain King had clean blankets, pillows, and washing materials all ready for them. They soon sat down to a dinner of ham, eggs, butter, pies, fresh buttermilk, and coffee. Along with the meal came two big pound cakes, provided by the two daughters just returned from school, with a note that said, "Compliments of the two Miss Kings to the McNelly Rangers."[49]

Although Ella and Alice had returned to the ranch in 1875, they were sent off to school again, this time to Mrs. Cuthbert's Young Ladies' Seminary in St. Louis. Mrs. Eugene Cuthbert, the principal, reported that the corps of teachers was good, the range of study extensive, and the domestic arrangements ample.[50] Alice made many good friends there, including Pearl "Lizzie" Ashbrook. Alice's older brother, Richard, had been making frequent trips to St. Louis to pursue his courtship of her. Alice excelled at Mrs. Cuthbert's seminary, graduating as class salutatorian. She had returned to South Texas shortly before Robert Kleberg accepted Captain King's invitation to visit the rancho.[51]

One day during that visit, the captain drove Robert out to see some of his holdings. Captain King rode on the spring seat of a light buckboard hitched to a matching team when he toured the ranch. Next to his seat, the captain always had his demijohn of Rosebud bourbon and a Winchester rifle. His usual driver was Willie Rawlinson, who was brought to the ranch to live when he was an eleven-year-old orphan. One wonders if Captain King was trying to help out a young orphan since he had been apprenticed out himself at a young age and had to make it on his own. On the ranch, the captain could be domineering one minute or acting like he was just one of the workers the next. He loved to play pranks on the Kineños but also would work side by side with them, building fences or hammering away in the blacksmith forge. There was a bond of loyalty between them that would last for generations. Young Robert would have to earn that loyalty for himself one day.[52]

During their long drive together, Captain King may have explained to young Kleberg what a difficult time he and the other ranchers were having due to the drought. Rain had been sparse, and the grass had already started to wither. King had a heavy investment to protect; he had pursued a policy of upgrading the quality of his stock, both cattle and horses, at every opportunity. The captain was also facing other problems, such as barbed wire fences cutting across the old routes to the railroad sidings, previously open ranges closing, and the outbreak of "Texas fever," a disease that seemed to appear in northern herds after contact with Texas cattle. As a result, northern cattlemen would halt the northbound Texas herds with armed guards, thus enforcing "Winchester Quarantines."[53]

Returning from a long day riding the vast pastures, King and Kleberg were met with warmth and hospitality as they drove up to the low-slung plantation home on the rise of the vast estate. During Robert's five-day visit, he had an opportunity to visit with the family and enjoy their company. Alice would tell their children in later years that she had known it was "love at first sight" when she laid eyes on the young lawyer—and his mustache.[54]

Robert Kleberg was described as "a stockily built man, a little below medium stature. His complexion was ruddy and he wore a bushy mustache the same sandy brown color as the thick shock of curly hair that crowned him. His blue eyes were usually mild and often merry—but they could level with a glint bearing sharp authority. . . . His spirit and manner were lively. Fond of company, he enjoyed good stories, told them well, and he loved to sing[,] especially the old German songs learned from his mother." He was undoubtedly welcome and delightful company for the shy Alice.[55]

From that visit forward, there began "a most exceedingly proper,

After Robert Justus Kleberg Sr. defeated Captains Richard King and Mifflin Kenedy in a lawsuit, King was impressed with him and invited the young man to visit his rancho. It was there that Robert first laid eyes on his future wife, Alice King. Corpus Christi Public Libraries, Corpus Christi, Texas.

unhurried and fond Victorian courtship" between the cultivated young lawyer and the "cattleman's winsome youngest daughter."[56]

A Young Lawyer Establishes Himself

ROBERT RETURNED TO Corpus Christi by train from the Rancho Santa Gertrudis with a good deal to contemplate. Perhaps his thoughts were full of the vast frontier empire he had just visited, but his subsequent correspondence suggests that he was more likely thinking of the youngest daughter, with her "deep brown eyes and silken tresses."[57] Robert had recently joined a law firm with Samuel Lackey and Robert Stayton, thus becoming the firm of Stayton, Lackey, and Kleberg, headquartered in Victoria with a branch in Corpus Christi, and the firm received a five-thousand-dollar annual retainer from Captain King.[58]

It was a good time to be in Corpus Christi. Civic energy and excitement were being generated by no other than Captain Richard King, Captain Mifflin Kenedy, and Mr. Uriah Lott. Corpus Christi had long dreamed of a way to connect the harbor and its shipping to the emerging trade in Mexico. There was an active cart business, but the city's business community also wanted a railroad connection to the border to capture the profitable trade with Mexico and bypass the Brownsville and Matamoros connection.

The project of completing a railroad from Corpus Christi to Laredo had been a challenging job, both financially and logistically. King, Kenedy, and Lott had united their efforts and begun to seek financial support in March 1875. In November 1876 the first portion of track was laid in Corpus Christi with great fanfare and the placing of a gilded spike that looked like gold; it was promptly stolen.[59] The project met with many obstacles along the way, however. For example, when two of the major investors, brothers James and Andrew Dull of Harrisburg, Pennsylvania, came to Corpus Christi to inspect the project because it was behind schedule and over budget, they traveled to the end of the twenty-five-mile rail route and were met by robbers. The thieves took all of their valuables, turned over their carriage, stole their horses, stripped them to their underwear, and left them bound hand and foot to mesquite trees.[60] In 1881, six years after beginning the venture, King, Kenedy, and Lott sold their interest to General William Jackson Palmer, president of the Denver & Rio Grande Railroad, for $5 million, with the three men making a total profit of $483,174.52.[61]

All over Corpus Christi, members of the business community and their social circles toasted their success and the completion of the rail line to Laredo. Lott, the builder, promoter, and manager, received a seventy-piece silver tea service from appreciative citizens. In turn, Lott presented King with a bronze sculpture of a pit bull dog, perhaps for his tenacity, and to Kenedy he gave a telescope, to symbolize his vision. Captains King and Kenedy also planned an extravaganza—a private excursion for 150 hand-selected guests who would travel the newly completed rail line from Corpus Christi to Laredo.[62]

Robert Kleberg received one of the 150 coveted invitations; his connection with the King family was already paying off. On October 2, 1881, Robert Kleberg described the celebratory rail excursion in a letter to his sister:

Last Tuesday Captains King & Kenedy, the great stockmen, . . . gave a free excursion to many of their friends—on the first passenger train to Laredo. They provided plenty to eat and drink for their guests—to give you an idea of the splendor & style in which it was carried on[,] I will tell you that over forty baskets of champagne, some two thousand cigars and plenty of other liquors were furnished by them to be drank on the way—the consequence was that quite a number of our leading citizens & Pillars of the church were perfectly exhausted with pleasure by the time they reached Laredo. The excursion train returned the next day but as I had some business I remained over in Laredo—& while there went across the river into Mexico, where I stayed over during one night—the trip was quite interesting to me, as it was the first time that I have been outside of the United States.[63]

As Robert Kleberg noted in his letter, most of the prominent men in Corpus Christi and the surrounding area were on the train with him. A poem written during the trip and attributed to Judge James O. Luby provides an interesting look at the leading citizens of Robert's community and on the way they enjoyed themselves on the trip.

The King-Kenedy Excursion to Laredo

September twenty seventh, eighteen eighty one,
Will long be remembered for pleasure and fun,
When the guests all arrived before setting sun,
At the City of Laredo,
Ed Williams, the Ledger upheld in its might,
Eli Merriman the Free Press' shining light,
And of inside matter they took in a sight,
On the Excursion to Laredo.
D. Mac. Turner, Stanley Welch and McCampbell, too,
With John Givens and Scott of the jolly crew,

The scenery through glasses oft did view,
On the Excursion to Laredo.
Davis the banker from his seat didn't budge,
Sat there quite sober, as Russell the judge,
Against the drought had an evident grudge,
On the Excursion to Laredo
Alfred Evans then to a point of order arose,
While addressing the guests in classic pose,
On Allen Davis's sombrero he skinned his nose,
On the Excursion to Laredo

Judge Peyton Smythe, the political purifier,
With his waving cane in hand awe did inspire,
Having taken it straight with his wonted fire,
On the Excursion to Laredo
Amongst us a Plato we had, but no Aristotle,
Of difficult essay or problems to throttle,
While of course totally ignoring the bottle,
On the Excursion to Laredo
With the Medical Corps Hamilton quietly sat,
Doctor Spohn on the drum played rat-ta-tat,
Doctor Turpin mourning the loss of his hat,
On the Excursion to Laredo
For diversified fun, we all had to thank,
That genial whole-souled Louis DePlanque,
You wouldn't catch him with an empty tank,
On the Excursion to Laredo.
Though no vocalist, William Woodpecker Wright,
Gave us warbling ditties airy and bright,
And W-6 with acclaim was voted "All Right,"
On the Excursion to Laredo
Though some their liquids ne'er renigged [reneged],
Still against others the fates were leagued,
John Woessner for instance got fatigued,
On the Excursion to Laredo

John Swisher on fun bent was just red hot,
Ably seconded by the rollicky William Lott,
Always willing to repeat right on the spot,
On the Excursion to Laredo
Doc DeRyee and the Bishop were quiet and staid,
Wondering who put the stick in the lemonade
While Thomas on the symbals [*sic*] vigorusly [*sic*] played,
On the Excursion to Laredo
Fitzsimmons, Don Reuben and Captain Greer,
Old-timers three and full of good cheer,
The deacons and vestrymen hysted [hoisted] the bear,
On the Excursion to Laredo
The heat was so sultry, caused sugar to melt,
But that didn't matter to George Westervelt,
And at comforting the weary he took the belt,
On the Excursion to Laredo
The Wrights, Adamses and Hobbses were in force,
And Reynolds from Palos Ventanas of course,
The Corpus Quartet from singing got hoarse,
On the Excursion to Laredo
Long Life to Captain King and Kenedy, too,
And Col. Hungerford who put us safely through,
To all of them our lasting thanks are due,
For our pleasant trip to Laredo

San Diego, Texas,
Sept. 28, After the Ball[64]

A few days after returning from the rail excursion, a political appointment changed the status of Robert's law firm, Stayton, Lackey and Kleberg. On November 2, 1881, Governor Oran M. Roberts appointed Judge John Stayton an associate justice of the Texas Supreme Court to fill a resigning justice's unexpired term. It was a surprise to Stayton, a relatively unknown small-town lawyer. Judge Stayton went on to be elected to a six-year term, was promoted to chief justice, and served in that capacity until his death in 1894. He was described as "calm, forceful, highly capable, and able to stand 'four square to every wind that blew.'"[65] Robert Kleberg wrote to his father on November 30, 1881, telling him that much of the law firm's business in Corpus Christi had been left solely to Robert. He told his father that he felt a great sense of duty to handle the business properly.

As Robert began taking on more responsibility at the law firm, Corpus Christi began growing and generating more business. By 1885 the population had reached forty-two hundred, and the town had three banks, a customs house, railroad machine shops, an ice factory, carriage factories, and several hotels. Captain Kenedy had announced that he was buying a lot on the high bluff overlooking the bay and was going to build a home and move to Corpus Christi, and years later, after the captain's death, Henrietta King also built a home on the bluff so that Alice and Robert's children could go to school in town. Corpus Christi also gained Episcopal, Presbyterian, Methodist, Catholic, and Baptist churches.[66] Captain and Mrs. Mifflin Kenedy helped fund construction of the Catholic church, and Captain and Mrs. King helped fund the building of the Presbyterian church. As Robert's business and legal responsibilities increased, his social profile followed suit. He was an attractive young bachelor, and Corpus Christi was full of social activities. Promenading along the bay was popular, and a pavilion on the beach was the scene of dances and socials. Billiards was a common pastime for both men and women, as were dances, which often included the quadrille, the minuet, the polka, the waltz, and the schottische. Popular music included modern Mexican folk songs and Irish ballads, with Robert's favorites being tunes brought by German-speaking settlers: "Deutschland, Deutschland, über alles" and "Heil Direin Siegerkranz," sung to the melody of "America." Hunting was another favorite pastime, mostly for men, their quarry being rabbits, doves, and other species in a vast array of fowl and game.[67]

In February 1882, Captain King suffered a major personal and business setback when his longtime friend and lawyer, Stephen Powers, died. The captain wrote to Powers's partner, Jim Wells, in

Brownsville, Texas, that his friend's death "is a great loss to all of us" and that "you must double your energy in all particulars and . . . fill my dear friend's place. There is not a man in this State, less yourself, misses him more than myself. God bless him and his dear family."[68] Captain King and Judge Powers had met thirty years earlier, when the captain was shipping goods on the Rio Grande, and now he was asking Powers's law partner to continue representing him. King soon traveled to Brownsville to discuss his business with Wells and to meet with his banker, Francisco Yturria. The young lawyer Wells wanted to know how often the captain required reports on his legal matters, and the captain said with strong purpose, "Young man, the only thing I want to hear from you is when I can move my fences."[69] Mifflin Kenedy's wife Petra also felt a deep sense of loss at Powers's death and had the new bells they had given to the Catholic church in Corpus rung in his honor.[70] Through the years, Robert worked frequently with Jim Wells, who would one day become his law partner.

The death of Judge Powers was not the only crisis Captain King and his ranching empire faced in the early 1880s. Drought had settled over the land in 1881 and persisted in 1882. In July 1882 there was more bad news from Rancho Santa Gertrudis when Henrietta King's half brother Bland Chamberlain, who had grown up on the ranch, died at the age of thirty-three. He came down with a fever while working under the hot sun and grew delirious, calling out for the captain, who had been like a father to him. Captain King hurried home when he heard of the young man's fever, and when he got to Bland's bedside, the captain asked if he knew who it was speaking to him. Bland replied, "Yes, El Cojo," and he promptly died.[71] Bland's death must have been hard on Alice King because they had grown up together.

Alice knew there were other troubles at the rancho. Her sister Ella had just had a baby, Henrietta Mary King Welton, born on July 7, 1882, in St. Louis, only seven months after Ella's marriage to Louis Morris Welton.[72] Henrietta King had been spending considerable time with Ella in St. Louis, thus leaving Alice to tend to her duties at the rancho and to take care of her father, whose health was beginning to fail. His

Petra Vela Kenedy, the wife of Mifflin Kenedy, provided Captains Kenedy and King with a link to the landed families and commerce in the Rio Grande region. She and Mifflin were lifelong friends of Richard and Henrietta King. Raymondville Historical Museum, Raymondville, Texas.

powerful body that had once been so full of energy was tired most of the time, and not even sleep could refresh him. At first he blamed the problems on his age, which was fifty-eight. Alice began to suspect otherwise when he admitted that his stomach hurt, it was hard to swallow, his gullet burned, and he was no longer hungry. To kill the pain, he used his Rosebud whiskey, but now he had to drink more of it to bring relief.[73]

The ranch itself was also in trouble because of the persistent heat and drought. King's good friend Captain Kenedy had just sold his ranch, Los Laureles, for $1.1 million to a Scottish syndicate and was buying another ranch, La Parra, which was closer to Corpus Christi and had water.[74] The captain began to wonder if he should look into selling his own ranch.

Robert continued to make trips out to the rancho to consult with the captain. On such trips, Robert and Alice had long visits together and grew closer. Robert also began to feel more at home. The house itself was filled with treasures. There were books, unique artwork, and religious ornaments. Many of these items had been obtained from blockade runners during the Civil War. French and English agents also brought goods from around the world. In the vast rooms of the ranch house there were regional treasures as well—Mexican silverware, pottery, embroidery, Aztec relics, rare carvings, weapons, and costly vessels. There was even a Watteau fan that had once belonged to Empress Carlota of Mexico during the Napoleonic monarchy there, as well as one of the ten gold pieces that Emperor Maximilian gave to the firing squad that executed him.[75]

Sometimes Alice traveled to Corpus Christi herself. She had joined the First Presbyterian Church there in 1882, which her parents had helped to build.[76] In April Uriah Lott had approached the Kings about donating the lot in back of the church facing Carancahua Street for a parsonage, and by July 1882 they had agreed to do that.[77]

On January 21, 1883, Robert's law firm published its business card in the *Corpus Christi Caller,* the newspaper that resulted from the consolidation of the *Free Press* and *Sunday Morning Ledger.*[78] The advertisement for business was perhaps a clue that Robert was worrying about his personal state of affairs. On February 12, 1883, he wrote to his father, telling him that he had been sick and was feeling weak and that his financial matters had not improved; he was almost out of money. He had no collections, but he was hoping to do better.[79]

Tragedy Strikes

WHILE ROBERT WAS DEALING with the difficulties in his law practice, Alice and her family received a disastrous blow. In late February 1883, Captain King received a telegram that his youngest son, nineteen-year-old Lee, was gravely ill with pneumonia. He was living at the Southern Hotel in St. Louis while furthering his education. Henrietta and her son Richard immediately left for St. Louis, while Alice stayed behind with her father. Lee died at two o'clock in the morning on March 1, 1883. Jim Wells wrote to Mifflin Kenedy that he had arrived at Rancho Santa Gertrudis about three o'clock in the afternoon on that day to find the family in deep grief over the death of Lee. Wells said that the captain and Alice were heartbroken, and then he asked Mifflin if perhaps it would be better for the captain and Alice to go to St. Louis to be with the family for a while. Wells felt that, because of Mifflin's closeness to the family, he should suggest it.[80]

The St. Louis newspaper reporting on Lee's death stated that he was supplementing his liberal education with a commercial course in order to prepare for a business career.[81] Captain King had intended that career to be the running of his rancho and the family's business affairs. After all, this was the son who loved the rancho and the land and who knew the livestock, the grass, and the water. According to the newspaper, Captain King and his daughter Alice were present at the burial. Lee's death had broken his father's heart, and his mother became seriously ill and remained in St. Louis for months.[82] It was left to Alice to accompany her father home, take care of him, and try to hold Rancho Santa Gertrudis together.

The captain and Alice were back at the rancho by March 18, and in his subsequent correspondence with Henrietta, he told her that he could not write to her with "any heart."[83] Petra Kenedy also wrote to Henrietta to convey her family's condolences and express her understanding of this great loss and her hope that, with God's help, Henrietta and Captain King would be consoled in their grief. Petra understood all too well the loss of a young son; Petra and Mifflin had lost their youngest son, Willie, seven years earlier, when he was almost the same age that Lee was at his death.[84] King soon wrote to Henrietta again, this time saying that he was tired of the business and wanted to quit and spend the balance of his time quietly. He wrote her again to ask if she wanted to sell or keep her cattle and sheep. He advised selling them for cash; he may have had a prospective buyer. On April 15, 1885, the *New Orleans Times Democrat* reported that Captain King had an asking price of $6.5 million for his rancho and stock.[85] Henrietta returned home on May 2 and wrote to Mifflin Kenedy that Captain King was not well; she was writing on his behalf to say that he needed Captain Kenedy to send him a check for twenty-five thousand dollars. Captain King's ever-present Rosebud may have clouded the issue because, by the next day, he was writing to Kenedy that he had received his check.[86]

Two weeks later King wrote Kenedy that, because there was not enough grass, he was selling ten thousand cattle; he hated to sell the heifers. He next wrote to ask if Kenedy could help out Bland Chamberlain's widow by buying 150 of her cattle so that she could pay off some of Bland's debts. He soon wrote to Kenedy again, indicating that a group of agents was coming to assess the ranch; he asked Kenedy to come out for the day, although he feared there was really no point in doing so because he did not think they were serious about buying.[87] A notice in the *Corpus Christi Caller* on May 27, 1883, reported that Captain King and his daughter were in town; this trip may have been a meeting with the land agents.[88]

When the agents got to the rancho, they told Captain King that they wanted to start by seeing the cattle. Victor Alvarado, one of King's most trusted vaqueros, told the following story. Captain King ordered his men to have a roundup by nine the next morning, and King and the agents rode out to the roundup in his large black coach. The herd was so big they couldn't see it well, so they climbed on top of the coach to get a better view. Alvarado estimated that the herd comprised about twelve thousand head. The prospective buyers asked if he could gather larger herds, and King said he could gather four or five herds as large or larger than the one they had just seen. The agents then informed him that they couldn't buy the herd in front of them much less the land too, and they left with regret.[89]

During this time Robert Kleberg was involved in a very difficult lawsuit. A few years earlier, in 1879, Helen Chapman had filed suit against Captain King, claiming that she owned an undivided one-half interest in the original Rincón de Santa Gertrudis, as well as title to a separate 240-acre property held by King. Two law firms, M. Campbell & Givens and Lackey & Stayton, represented Mrs. Chapman, whose husband, Major William Warren Chapman, had died in 1859. In 1881, Robert had joined the latter firm and participated in representing her. At the same time, however, the law firm was also representing Captain King on various issues. Captain King claimed that Major Chapman verbally and later by letter surrendered his interest in both deeds to King in forgiveness of his debt for the purchase price but that the letter was lost when Union forces raided his ranch during the Civil War. On April 7, 1883, four years after the suit was filed, the parties settled Cause no. 1279. Helen Chapman, who had moved to South Carolina, died in late 1881, and the courts awarded her estate, with consent of both parties (through her executor, John Rankin), $5,811.75 for its interest in the Rincón and title to the separate 240 acres.

Helen Chapman's son, William B. Chapman, was dissatisfied with the settlement, and on May 21, 1883, he wrote Robert that he was opposed to allowing King to take judgment for the property. The Chapman heirs continued to be unhappy with the ruling and the fact that Robert's law firm represented both clients in legal matters. The family continued to pursue the case for more than a century; it was finally settled before the Supreme Court of Texas on August 28, 2003.[90]

As time went on, Robert Kleberg also began handling Mifflin Kenedy's business affairs. As Alice was growing up, Mifflin Kenedy was like an uncle to her, and he and her father were perhaps even closer than brothers. So Robert took it upon himself to look after Kenedy as an extended family member. In 1883, however, it was Kenedy who came to the rescue of King, and it was under very stressful circumstances.

By the middle of June that year, the sale of the rancho had fallen through, and King was in a desperate situation. The rancho was out of water. He had placed five thousand cattle at a tank, and Dr. Spohn had told his father-in-law, Mifflin Kenedy, that if it did not rain within a week the cattle would die. Captain King had written to Mifflin Kenedy's son James at La Parra and asked if he could let his cattle into the ranch so that they could have access to his lakes. That request set off a series of letters between James and his father on the condition of their cattle and how long they could last without rain. Captain Kenedy finally wrote to Captain King and told him that, under the circumstances, it would be impossible for him to take any of his cattle. He then wrote James and told him how concerned he was about King. He wanted to help him, but it was too late, and if he did take King's cattle they would both probably lose their herds and go down together. Even though they were not blood brothers, the old saying that blood is thicker than water applies here: two days later Mifflin Kenedy wrote Richard King that he had permission to turn loose five thousand head at two of his lakes, and, if he didn't hear otherwise from him, he would give permission for another five thousand on Saturday. He simply could not turn his back on his friend.[91]

A Friendship Deepens

THE RAINS FINALLY CAME. Henrietta was away from home again, and Captain King wrote to her that the grass was green once more on the lawn. On July 4 there was a celebration at the ranch, and Captain King dusted off the cannons from his old steamboats and fired them in honor of both the holiday and the rain.[92] It turned out that Captain King, Henrietta, and Alice had even more to celebrate in July. Richard II became engaged to marry Alice's classmate and good friend Pearl "Lizzie" Ashbrook in December. The Kings found this match very desirable, unlike the matches of Alice's older sisters. Henrietta (Nettie) had married Major E. B. Atwood of the US Army Quartermaster Department on November 23, 1878, in an elaborate ceremony at the Lindell Hotel in St. Louis, where, it was reported, the bride received gifts worth more than ten thousand dollars. In contrast, Ella had married Louis M. Welton, a merchant of St. Louis and San

Antonio, in a quiet ceremony at the ranch.[93] In honor of Richard's marriage, Captain and Mrs. King presented the young couple on July 15, 1883, by deed and gift, a forty-thousand-acre well-watered ranch: Rancho Puerta de Agua Dulce. Young Richard and Lizzie were married at her grandmother's home in Wentzville, Missouri, on December 12, 1883. They left after the ceremony for a honeymoon in the East, and when they arrived in Texas in January, there was an elegant new home waiting for the new Mrs. King.[94] Alice and Robert were good friends with Lizzie and Richard through the years. Richard and Lizzie bought out an heir to the old Ashbrook farm near St. Louis, and they spent their summers there strengthening the Kings' St. Louis connections. Young Richard had a different view of ranching than his father and converted some of his pastures to growing cotton, but sometimes Captain King had to bail him out financially.

Alice and Robert's relationship had grown closer and closer during the last two years of their courtship. They had dinner conversations with the captain and Henrietta and their guests in the outdoor dining area and afterward in the parlor, where everyone gathered for music and singing. The couple took leisurely walks beside Santa Gertrudis Creek and sat on the covered verandah with the night breezes cooling their faces. Robert visited the ranch in August with some of his friends, and, afterward, Alice wrote him the following letter on August 30, 1883:

Mr. Kleberg—
Kind Friend.

Again 'tis a pleasing duty to acknowledge my indebtedness, I feel, I can
No other answer make but thanks
And thanks & ever oft good turns
Are shuffled off with such uncurrent pay.

Papa left this afternoon, for Brownsville, much to my regret. I can't tell you how much we enjoyed the brief visit of your friends. I was charmed with the Judge—as to your "other Mother," suffice it to say, she is all my "fancy painted" her.[95]

Assuring you the grapes will not go a-begging,

With kind regards from Mother, & a multiplicity of thanks from

Your sincere friend,

A. G. King[96]

Robert had thus had the opportunity to share the hospitality of the rancho with his friends. Captain King was pleased with Robert's work as a lawyer, and he and Henrietta apparently had no objections to him courting their youngest daughter. He was winning over not only the girl with the dark brown eyes but also her parents.

In the fall, Captain King was recovering from his financial difficulties and wrote Mifflin Kenedy a letter of thanks for lending him money in August; he told his friend that he could never repay him for his good business advice and other things. Also that month, Captain King was very busy with his ice business in Brownsville; by early September the newspaper had reported that Captain King had been in town and there were hopes that King Ice Works might expand its business to include making ice cream and delivering it to residences.[97] November brought romantic news. John Kenedy, Mifflin and Petra's son, would be marrying in New Orleans in January, and James, another Kenedy son, had married Corina Ballí on November 2.[98] On November 4 the Corpus Christi newspaper reported that "Mrs. King, Richard King Jr., [*sic*] Alice, and Miss Pearl Ashbrook, a lady from St. Louis, were in town and had returned to Santa Gertrudis. Rumor is that he will not return alone."[99]

As the year came to a close, Alice drew even closer to her parents as well as to Robert. The captain wrote of his youngest daughter, "She is a little lady in all things and so good I could not do without my little Pet." More and more as her mother was absent from the ranch, Alice was her father's companion and her mother's agent charged with watching over her father and trying to curtail the captain's increasingly hard drinking. On one occasion, Alice added a postscript to a letter written by her father: "Mama precious one, wanted to write you tonight but Papa wants me to read to him, so all I can do is to send a heart full of loving thoughts to the dear absent ones, Papa came home today.—All right and as well as when he left, bless his heart."[100] Alice was trying to keep her father as sober as possible or "all right," fill in for her mother as the hostess for the rancho, and still enjoy the ever-growing relationship with the ruddy, handsome, and intelligent lawyer, Robert Kleberg.

The Love Letters, 1884–1887

IF WE ARE TO BELIEVE the letters of Robert Justus Kleberg Sr. to Alice Gertrudis King (and, after reading them, who could not believe?), when he met Alice he fell deeply in love with this child of a larger-than-life Irish sea captain and the refined Southern daughter of a Presbyterian minister. The Kleberg-King union must have been a marriage of great love, for this cache of Victorian love letters reveals a man at times seemingly besotted with ardor. They also provide a glimpse of the Victorian-era world in which these two moved and the people and events of their lives from April 12, 1884, to August 17, 1887.

My Dear Little Heart

[Addressed to] Miss Alice King at Santa Gertrudis,
Collins P.O.[1], Nueces Co. Texas

Corpus Christi April 18
Friday 12, C. W. [sic] 1884
My Dear Little Heart

This is a good time of the night to begin writing an answer to your kind and interesting letter of day before yesterday—I received it last night and was tempted to answer it [at] once in order to give vent to my emotions in some way but I thought that would be almost too prompt an answer, that you could hardly submit to an affliction of this kind so frequently, so I simply took myself to my lonely room and there indulged in quiet reflection over the future, the present, and the past until I unconsciously found myself dreaming instead of thinking—dreaming of you, my little Darling, dreams so happy that the only regret they bring is that they are dreams and not reality. Yet I have the consolation of having enjoyed that happiness even if it is but imaginary—I cannot tell you, my little heart, with what emotions your candid expression of your love for me filled me. It fills my breast with pride and my soul with a peace that I never before experienced. I feel that I have won forever the greatest and most precious prize that man can win—the unreserved and never dying love of a true and pure woman—but every attempt at describing, in expressing in words my feelings, proves but too plainly that is not the way to do it. I hope that I may be able to give better evidences of it than that.

I only wish, my little darling, that I could help you bear your troubles better. Rest assured that [I] appreciate your confiding them to me, and that you certainly have my sympathy. I hope that someday I can take some of them on my shoulders. They are better fitted for burdens than yours, and are more accustomed to their weight—and remember, my little heart, that all these troubles will make us appreciate the blessing we enjoy now and that may be in store for us in the future evermore—

The troubles to which Robert was referring would include the aftermath of Robert E. Lee King's death on March 1, 1883, in St. Louis. Alice's mother was still in St. Louis at this time, so Alice was thus in charge of tending to her father.[2]

I am sorry that I have not been able to see you before now but unexpected business will detain me until next week when I hope to be at Santa Gertrudis. I have been busily engaged in consummating a sale of Mrs. Rogers' Ranch and cattle in this county to the Mr. Rachal. It is quite a little piece of work but I shall finish it next Tuesday when I will have to go out to the Rabb Ranch to close up the transaction—but these matters do not interest you nor do I think much of them when my thoughts turn to you. It seems true now that I would give all these days that I am spending away from you for one sweet kiss from my own little heart.

Martha Rabb Rogers—"The Cattle Queen of Texas"—had married Methodist minister C. M. Rogers, who quickly went through her fortune, forcing the sale of the ranch in 1884. The buyer, Rachal, later sold it to the Driscolls. The oil later discovered on the ranch became the basis for the Driscoll family fortune.[3]

I received a letter tonight from my brother telling me of my sister's safe arrival in Galveston. How I wish I could be with my mother when she meets her, for they never expected to see each other again—both being in feeble health and so far apart—God bless the railroads for bringing us nearer those whom we love far away.

The brother to whom Robert referred was in all likelihood Marcellus E. Kleberg, attorney, who lived in Galveston at the time this letter was written.[4] Robert's mother was Rosalie von Roeder Kleberg, a Texas pioneer.[5] The daughter whom Rosalie was awaiting in Galveston was likely Clara Hillebrand.[6]

Yes, my little Darling, the time will come when none can say that they are happier than we, not even Richard and his dear little wife. I think that we will spend some happy days together with them.

Robert was already looking forward to spending time with his future brother-in-law, Richard King II and his wife, Pearl "Lizzie" Ashbrook, Alice's former roommate at Mrs. Cuthbert's Seminary in St. Louis.

I have not had the pleasure of meeting Mr. [Rules?] yet. I think he has gone away with the Stuttz troop though I do not know. I have heard nothing of him.

The Stuttz troupe was an entertainment group that went from town to town presenting works such as *Faust* and *The Flying Dutchman.*[7] Mr. Rules may have been a member of the Stuttz troupe.

Don't let me look for [an] answer too long & tell me that you did not catch the Corpus Christi fever. It is said to be increasing. I feel splendidly now & shall take good care of myself.
Buenos Notches [sic] *(kiss) Your RJK*

Robert may have been referring to yellow fever, sometimes known as yellow jack, which was always a worry on the coast.[8]

[Addressed to] Miss Alice G. King at Santa Gertrudis, Collins, Nueces County

Corpus Christi
May 13th 1884
My Dear Little Heart—

I cannot tell you with how much anxiety I looked for the result of the mail last night. I felt so sure that I would get my letter, that I could not be disappointed, that I don't know what I should have done had I not soon gotten my letter. Especially have I longed for a word of encouragement since the beginning of this trial that seemed almost everlasting to me—And yesterday I felt so nervous that I could scarcely speak without betraying it as some very important questions arose during the trial. It was the hardest and most disagreeable work I ever did—to arise—and speak against the interest of [a] friend and in favor of a man who cannot appreciate my position. No one but you can do that and it seems to me that the other attorney in the case with me made it convenient that I should fight all the hard fights. Well today was the final day of this trial, the entire day being consumed with the arguments of the lawyers in the case. I had to make the closing speech to show that my friend's lawyers were mistaken in their positions & that their arguments were wrong and then finally show the defects of their case & the strength of my own. The court gave the law in favor of Mr. Collins. The case was then submitted to the jury of twelve men and they have not at this hour 9½ returned a verdict. There is one Negro on the jury & I have heard that he is hanging the jury—the other 11 white men being in my favor. If the jury does not agree it will be a mistrial and the whole thing must be gone through with again, but I am not going to say another word about it now. I have bored you with too much of it already.

The *Corpus Christi Caller* of May 18, 1884, reports "the suit between Capt. R. King and N. G. Collins to try title to a piece of land in Duval County of about two leagues, which occupied the District court all last week, resulted in a verdict for Mr. Collins. The case is still before the court, and will no doubt go to Supreme Court." A league is 4,428.4 acres, so the suit concerns a dispute over almost 9,000 acres. Robert's anxiety comes from being in opposition to Richard King and thus fearful that the court's decision might affect his courtship of Alice.

Your good father is well but I fear much worried about the trial, of course. I hardly feel like going near him for he has been so kind and considerate towards me in this case. Now, my little darling, selfish fellow that I was, I have unburdened my troubles first and now I buried yours.

I certainly was decidedly astonished at what you tell me, to say the least, and I cannot bear with any degree of comfort or composure the thought of such a thing that someone should try to come between us, but rest assured it shall bring me the closer (if that is possible) to you and while I have your love & life none ever shall be able [to] separate me from you.

While I am speaking of this I will answer your little question about the change of our firm name with pleasure for it pleases me to know that you are interested in my affairs. The cause of the change is simply because Mr. Lackey, who is growing old and his health delicate and because he has accumulated sufficient property, desired to retire from practice entirely. That is all and it is a decided advantage to us, as he has not been able to give us but very limited assistance & our practice will remain the same—

The *Corpus Christi Caller* of May 18, 1884, also noted that "among those visiting the bluff city last week were Wm. Chamberlain of Brownsville; Hon. N. G. Collins, Chas. Hoffman and W. L. Franks, of San Diego." It also reported that "a change has been made in the law firm of Lackey, Stayton & Kleberg. The firm is now Stayton & Kleberg. See change in card." The card referred to is an advertisement in the newspaper.[9]

And [Little Norma?] is my little "adopted sister" & I shall always be as a brother to her and nothing more—the time has past [sic] *when I could love another than you—on you I have set all my hopes for happiness and I shall* not *change.*

I actually believe that I could be jealous of anyone who would try to win your affections from me. I can't stand too much of it and our mutual friend must not be too *attentive or I don't know how I would feel about it. I hardly know, my little heart, how to advise you as to the best course to pursue in the matter you speak of. I think your own good judgment & heart and true womanhood will be your best guide in the matter. I should think it best to let him know as soon as he makes any inquiries on the subject that such a thing is not to be thought of. Let his friend tell him and that will perhaps satisfy him.*

It is intriguing to wonder who might also have been trying to court Alice. She was certainly one of the most eligible single women in the area and the heiress to a fortune. Robert's letter seems to suggest that he felt threatened by the prospect of competition for Alice.

*I have a little peace [*sic*] of gossip to tell you. I met our friend Mrs. Dr. S the other evening out in front of the St. James. She was in the buggy while the Dr. had gone in. She called me up and congratulated me. When I told her she was too precocious she said that on that day your father had been at her mother's house & she told him that she understood we were engaged. Our conversation was interrupted about that time. I have not seen her since. I never saw such busy people about other people's affairs. This, however, is nothing new to me. I am getting used to it.*

"Mrs. Dr. S" was Sarah Kenedy Spohn. Captain King had visited Sarah's mother, Petra Vela Kenedy, and told her of Robert and Alice's engagement. At this point, Petra was already seriously ill with the cancer that would kill her in 1885.[10] Built in 1869 by J. T. James, the St. James Hotel, located at the corner of Lawrence and Chaparral streets, was the first major hotel in Corpus Christi.[11]

I don't know when I will be able to see you. I hope soon. Good bye now for the present—and believe me, forever. Yours always. Good night.

❧

[Addressed to] Miss Alice G. King, Santa Gertrudis,
Collins P.O., Nueces Co., Texas

Corpus Christi May 18, 1884
My Dear Little Heart
I cannot imagine why I have not heard from you in so long unless it is because you are unwell—suffering with one of those dreadful spells of headaches. I do not want to ask you to write

After her marriage to Dr. Arthur Spohn, Sarah Kenedy Spohn was one of Corpus Christi's most prominent citizens. She is the "Mrs. Dr. S" in Robert's letters. Raymondville Historical Museum, Texas.

The St. James Hotel (left) was completed in 1870 and a landmark in Corpus Christi for many years. Known as a gathering place for cattlemen and traveling dignitaries, the St. James had back rooms where gamblers, lawyers (including Robert Kleberg), physicians, and ranchers played cards and billiards. Courtesy of Anita Eisenhauer.

to me if such is the case for I know that you will not let me wait any longer than you can help it.

Alice's headaches may have been stress-induced migraines.[12]

I felt sure last night that I would hear from you, but no. I got instead a little note from Mr. Welton acknowledging receipt of my last to him & in which his dear little wife & Little "Etta" send their regards. They are all well he writes.

Louis M. Welton was married to Ella Morse King, Alice's sister. The couple and their daughter, "Etta," lived in St. Louis.[13]

It cannot be that I have offended you in any way by anything contained in my last letter? I hardly remember what I wrote, for when I write to you I scribble down my thoughts just as they enter my head & heart without reflecting for a moment. Do not remain silent any longer if it is only a little note telling me that you will write to me soon. I will feel better. I cannot bear the thought that I have offended you. It troubles me so that I cannot write of anything else. Your father is well. I think the case will terminate Monday evening if not at least Tuesday evening.

The case Robert refers to is apparently the N. G. Collins suit, since Captain King is still in town attending it.

Just send me a little note if nothing more, and tell me, my little heart, what the trouble is.

Yours Sincerely
Robert J. Kleberg

[Addressed to] Miss Alice G. King, Santa Gertrudis, Collins P.O., Nueces Co., Texas

Corpus Christi May 27, 1884

My Dear Little Heart—

I did halfway expect to find a letter from you last Saturday, but since I got my letter last night I do not complain for it came just at the right time—a time when I would not have exchanged it for hardly anything else. It was just what I wanted and needed at that time—and its contents was the consolation I needed more than anything else. I cannot thank you enough for the sympathy and encouragement you expressed in it for me, for as long as I have your approval, your respect and your love, I can stand all else however hard the blow may be.

You will have learned the result of the trial before now from your father. We had a hard contest, every point in the case during the trial being contested in all these contests. Mr. Collins' side was victorious. The case was given to the jury & was zealously contested by both parties—as much if not more so than any case I ever participated in. The jury returned a verdict in favor of Mr. Collins. The judge, in writing out his instructions to the jury upon the law applicable to the case, left out the words "five [years?] before." Upon this error of the court, a new trial was applied for by your father's lawyers who complained that this error might have influenced the jury in finding their verdict, and the court granted a new trial so the whole case will have to be tried over again. As this error if error it was [sufficiently?] was made by the judge & not by me, I do not feel that I am in the least to blame by my client and I am perfectly willing, I fear more than willing, that your father should have another chance at the case. When the judge rendered his decision giving a new trial, setting aside the verdict of the jury, your father's face changed, wearing a very perceptible smile so that

I could not resist from smiling myself from the bottom of my heart. It seemed to please him so that I for the moment enjoyed it nearly as much as he did, though it was against my side. I am perfectly satisfied so far with the exception that I do not think that your father understood my feelings in the matter & for that reason may feel hurt at my action though he treated me with all the consideration & respect that I could possibly ask. And I can truly assure you that during all his trials & disappointments he was very careful of himself not to drink too much. I made it a point to visit him often at his room to keep him from doing so if possible.

I did not do Mr. Collins justice in my last letter to you, probably because of the dislike I had for the case, for after the verdict was rendered he assured me of his appreciation of my situation in this matter & the manner in which I did my duty & as evidence, he said, of his appreciation he made me a present of five hundred dollars. When I told him that I had rather not have it & I would prefer to return my fee besides, if I was only out of the case.

N. G. Collins, whom Robert was defending in the trial, was a wealthy rancher and the founder of Collins Station. He also served as a senator in the Texas Legislature.

Yes, my Little Darling, your words of approval & consolation give me a thousand times more satisfaction than all the money in this world—and it repays me better for any trouble. I fear, my little Darling, that you are but too correct in your advice that it is better that I should not visit you now. Besides, I could not half enjoy it unless I knew that I was welcome in your father's house by him. I have never yet entered a man's house as a visitor unless I thought that I was welcome. And it would be hard for me to do so now. Besides it might make things worse than they are & I fear that if I should even feel & know that I was not welcome I do not know what I should do. So for the present, I shall take your advice for once *(?) follow your advice. At any rate I shall not attempt [to] turn the pages of life's book in that chapter until I hear again from you.*

There are few things that are covered by the veil of the future that we can know, are there? But there is one thing that I do know of the future and that is that my love for you can never & will never change no matter what other changes the future may reveal. And I also feel that no matter what may [be] written on the pages of this book of life that are yet unturned, that through it will be written that I have your love, my little Darling, and I can read them all through though they may be blotted with tears as long as I can find there to read something of your love. I too confess that I should read ahead of the story a little to see what the plot of it is. I cannot but think that there is a story for us found here in the future. How near or far I cannot even imagine—a time when we shall be happy, when our fondest hopes shall be realized. Do not look too gloomily at things as they are, but I will not turn your thoughts to your troubles.

The game bag is finished. Good news. The thought of it brings back happy memories of the past. How I wish I could sit by your side now and help (?) you with your fancy works. I don't think I would find fault with anything this evening, if I could only be with you.

Robert was an avid hunter, so a new game bag in which to carry his trophies would be a treat for him.

When I go away this time I will probably be gone for several weeks or more as I shall stay with my Father as long as I possibly can. He is not recovering as rapidly as I had hoped or anticipated. He [is] still confined to his bed & I know the time hangs heavy over him for he is naturally of a very active temperament and likes to move around.

Robert's father suffered a paralytic stroke a short time before his eighty-second birthday, which was September 10. The stroke occurred before August 9, 1884, as can be seen from the date of this letter. Robert's parents then moved into a house built for them on the ranch of their daughter and son-in-law, Caroline and Robert C. Eckhardt, located near Yorktown.[14]

I can't tell yet when I will be able to leave here as court is still in session. Besides, I have a heavy brief to prepare as soon as possible. I have been working at it until my thoughts kept turning to you so I stopped at the brief & began your letter. I hope that before I leave you will be able to tell me that I am as welcome at Santa Gertrudis as formerly. I don't [know] what I shall do. I shall leave to [go] by the Puerta for a happy hunting ground, I presume.

Puerta was the ranch of Alice's brother, Richard King II. La Puerta de Agua Dulce (The Door to the Agua Dulce) was terminology in local usage to designate the area west of Corpus Christi, in the vicinity of Agua Dulce Creek.[15]

I have not heard any more gossip or rumor. Perhaps if I go away for a while that it will die out.

The city is quite gay now [with] theatrical performances twice every week & musical concerts and dancing at the Pavillion once every week. This evening I was invited to participate in a sailing party—given for the benefit of some visitors from Monterrey, among them a beautiful little Mexican Señorita. She speaks English well and is playing havoc with the heart of the Corpus [dudes?]. I was afraid I could not stand the pressure so I remained in my office at work on my brief—writing to you. While I have promised to follow your advice I do not think that I can do without one letter a week anyway. Besides I cannot see the possible harm in this—

The performances to which Robert referred could have been the Stuttz troupe or another traveling troupe.

Goodby now & do not let me "bide" too long for a letter from my little Darling—Yours always and always RJK

❧

[Addressed] to Alice G. King, Santa Gertrudis,
Collins P.O., Nueces Co. Texas. [Mailed from Austin, Texas.]

Robert wrote this letter in Austin, where he was arguing a case at the state's Supreme Court.

Austin Tex. June 4th 1884
My Dear Little Heart,

This is strange looking paper to write you a letter on but it is either this or no letter until tomorrow for I neglected getting paper while the stationery stores were open & this is all I have in my room. I use this for writing briefs—which are afterwards printed.

I left Corpus Saturday morning very unexpectedly as I was called by telegram Friday that I was wanted in the Supreme Court to represent my Laredo land suit—so I could not wait to get my letters—Saturday, I enquired at Collins for letters, but the P.M. [post master] must have overlooked your letter as he told me there was none for me. I left instructions at Corpus to forward any letters and this evening your letter came. I thought of writing to you last night but reconsidered—thinking that I might be overdoing the thing to write so often.

Now, my little heart, while the surroundings are not particularly favorable for a little chat with you as I am in my room working at a brief, yet something I found out since receiving your letter [is] that there is no use in my trying to write at my brief until I give vent to a little spell of devotion to my little Dar-

ling. I was in Judge Stayton's room when he handed me your letter—it was sent in his care—and discussing with him what he should say in reply to a letter addressed to him by members of the bars from different portions of the state insisting on his not resigning and becoming a candidate for Congress. This matter disposed of, as you will see in the next Galveston News in a letter from Judge Stayton in reply, I betook myself to [a] comfortable seat in his room and to read my letter. I also received one at the same time from home telling me of my Father's gradual recovery, and I can assure you that after reading both, my peace of mind and heart was wonderfully improved.

Judge Stayton was John W. Stayton of Cuero, in whose office Kleberg had read history and law. Stayton was later chief justice of the Supreme Court of Texas.[16]

I am glad to hear that your father has expressed no ill feeling towards me. For it would grieve me very much to learn that I had offended one who has befriended me so much and whose respect and esteem I prize so highly and to whom I owe so much gratitude. Capt. Kenedy told me during the progress of the case that while the Capt. [King] had spoken harshly of all other attorneys in the case he had not said an unkind word about me—but I shall let this ever-lasting case rest now.

I am now engaged in trying before the supreme court this case which I tried and lost in Laredo this spring. It is a suit involving one hundred and fifty thousand acres of land—and if I am successful my fee will amount to over twenty thousand acres of the land. I shall try my best. The whole case turns upon dry questions of law, and the decision by the supreme court will in all probability be a final decision of the case either for me or against me. After receiving such a nice long letter from my little Heart I can work with redoubled courage and vigor. So if I lose this case it will not be your fault.

I can appreciate your feeling in the Russell matter. You have taken the right resolution. Tell him plainly and frankly the truth and he cannot blame you, but I know that you will do this without telling me for I think I am a sufficient Judge of human nature that whatever weakness you may possess, insincerity is not one of them. For sincerity is the natural constituent of a truthful and noble character, and I know too that judging by the little encouragement which you gave me that you cannot have given him much whom you did not love and I can also assure you that you need never fear that your affection for me will be unrequited, for my love for you has become a part of my very nature and existence, and will last as long as I do.

Apparently someone named Russell was pursuing Alice and she had asked for Robert's advice on how to respond. Robert mentioned her letter in his letter of May 13, 1884. The *Corpus Christi Caller* of August 31, 1884, provides a possible clue to the identity of the other suitor: "Robert Kleberg shooting with gun club—15 balls revolving trap—scored 8—J. C. Russell, District Attorney in Corpus Christi."

Ah, what would I give for a few moments with my little darling, that I might try to tell her how much I love her. I am again indulging in the vain effort to find relief in trying to give vent to my emotions but they fill my whole heart and soul so completely that to write it down in weak and in expression [sic] words can give but little relief.

When shall I see you is a question which I ask myself as often as I think of you. I will have to return from here to Corpus Christi before going home and I shall be strongly tempted to see you before I go home, but that shall be as you wish and think best. I think that I will be in Corpus by next Sunday, though I cannot tell for certain. If you answer me immediately on the receipt of this, address your letter in care of Judge J. W. Stayton, Austin Tex.

Some friends have just called to see me—students at the University here from De Witt Co.—boys whom I have known since they were children. So I must close and let them tell me of their University days and will have to tell them of mine.

So goodby and Buenos Notches. (Kiss) Yours alone

RJK

Home for Robert was Cuero in DeWitt County. The students visiting him were probably students at the University of Texas, which had been established recently; classes were being held by September 15, 1883. The School of Law was also open then, so it is likely Robert was discussing his University of Virginia law school experiences with the University of Texas law school students.[17]

[Addressed to] Miss Alice G. King,
Collins P.O., Santa Gertrudis, Nueces Co.

Corpus June 22 1884

My Dear Little Heart

You will hardly expect another letter from me this week, and I know that you deserve something better than an affliction of this kind, and the meanest of all is that I am going to be ungrateful enough to make the receipt of so beautiful a present from you the excuse for this otherwise inexcusable act of writing to you three times in one week—but I truly appreciate the little present so highly that I cannot help thanking you for it forthwith. It is just as I would have it, I can suggest no improvement upon its design, and I have been unable to find anything about [it] to criticize. It is just [a] game bag to my heart and if you are good at guessing you can probably tell that somebody's heart has been completely bagged and the meshes are so peculiarly woven & of such strong cords that the game will never get out of the bag.

I have just returned from a call at Major White's with Edwin. The Maj & wife are going out on the morning train to the Puerta to visit Mr. & Mrs. R. King, Jr. [sic] *and from there the Maj. is going to Santa Gertrudis. I almost promised to go out with him but I do not think I will [torn and illegible] morning.*

"Major" J. H. C. White became secretary of the Kenedy Pasture Company after the death of his predecessor, Edwin Mallory. White married Miss Fannie Mallory.[18] Edwin was probably Edwin Chamberlain, Henrietta King's youngest half brother. He had been raised on the King Ranch and had worked for Captain King.[19]

I fully intended starting to Santa Gertrudis this morning but [it] began raining very heavily here about 6½ and continued for some time & I feared the heavy road & the swollen streams so I sent my horses back to the stable & I have instead spent the day here. Edwin has been with me until just now—ever since this morning early.

I was out taking tea last night when he came in & did not learn that he was in town until after he had retired. I am now revolving the plan in my mind that I will start tomorrow after noon—taking Edwin with me if it doesn't rain again in the morning. If it does I don't know what I will do. One thing is certain, I never wanted to see you my little Darling as much as I do now. Let this be an excuse for these frequent afflictions upon you—and another thing is certain, that I am going to see you just as soon as I can, so you can take warning that I may be before you, before you know it.

Do you know that night before last I went to the post office with a full expectation to find your letter & I am sure I had no reason to expect it except that I just felt that I was bound to have it and could not stand to be disappointed. But now I am going to end [torn and illegible] of you & [torn and illegible]

Buenos Notches. I will see you soon & [pray?] that you are well. Goodbye (kiss) RJK

❧

[Addressed to] Miss Alice G. King, Santa Gertrudis, Collins, Texas

Corpus Christi
July 6, 1884
My Dear Little Heart

This is a little late to begin a chat with you—(eleven o'clock) but I think I will sleep better after writing to you tonight and I fear if you had to read this tonight that it would have a narcotic effect upon you—but this will not reach you until about 2½ PM tomorrow—just about the time you will want to take your little nap, and this will come just in time.

I had quite a time going home the other day—I could not keep my eyes open for about half the way and the result was that I did not drive very fast during that time and when I finally awoke I saw some plovers and though it was then getting late, I could not resist the temptation to shoot a few. The result was that I did not reach town until about 9 o'clock—after supper hour. Imagine my feelings—all the hotels closed for supper and I as hungry as a wolf. The city was crowded with Laredo Excursionists.[20] *They were moving toward the Pavillion to lunch and to dance. I at once joined the throng of the pleasure seekers, and in a few moments I found myself paying my compliments to the lunch, and having satisfied the inner man I "took in" the dance for an hour or two, and at 12 oclock I was the most willing man to sleep you ever heard of and in a few moments I was on the Santa Gertrudis (with my dear little heart) dreaming over the near past, and in the morning I arose in fine spirits & health expecting to do much work during the day but it should not be so.*

Shortly after dinner I was called upon by two ladies to join

them at a moonlight pick-nick that evening on the bay shore and when they spoke of the nice lunch they were going to have I was too weak to resist the temptation and I accepted their invitation. Mrs Spohn and Miss Loveniskold were the ladies. I thought of the scheme I had mentioned to you. I at once asked Miss Lovenskiold to accompany me to the picnic ground and I think I have pretty well succeeded in starting my interested friend on a new track. I drove through the many streets of the city, by Mrs Doddridge, giving her a full benefit, and during the evening acted the gallant so well that Mrs. S. has become decidedly doubtful as to the true state of affairs. I have heard from them today. Gossip now "says" that I have taken a new departure, something must have gone wrong elsewhere with me, & etc. I think I shall now leave the city while this impression is abroad & perhaps they will let you rest for a little while.

Robert clearly was playing with Sarah Spohn and the other ladies of Corpus Christi, teasing them by driving through town with one other than his supposed intended, attending picnics, and having lunch. His ploy was evidently to mislead the ladies. Miss Lovenskiold would have been the daughter of Oscar C. Løvenskiold, a prosperous merchant and mayor of Corpus Christi.[21] Mrs. Doddridge is Rachel, wife of Perry Doddridge, merchant and banker, who worked for Mifflin Kenedy and Company in Brownsville in 1852. Doddridge was very involved with the development of transportation in South Texas, including various railway projects. Richard King considered him a great friend and adviser and named him an executor of his will.[22]

Well, so much for foolishness, my little Darling. On my return I found a letter from Robt. Stayton telling me that he would be in Corpus Christi on Wednesday so I shall not leave here until I have seen him—it seems that one thing after another postpones my trip.

Last night Judge Murphy died. He was buried today. He died very suddenly while he was eating his supper his [head] dropped upon his breast & his life was gone. I attended his funeral this evening. His poor wife seems hardly able to bear the weight of grief—& yet it was doubtless best—for her for him———

Judge Murphy was John Bernard Murphy, lawyer and politician. He was mayor of Corpus Christi from 1880 until 1884, when poor health forced him to resign. Shortly after his resignation, he died, on July 4, 1884.[23]

I sent the medicine your mother wanted & also the gun I took from the ranch—to Collins by tomorrow's train

This evening since tea I called on Capt Kenedy. He is unwell—so I spent the evening with him. I have just returned from there now. He is suffering from some irritation of the ileus. Nothing serious but annoying to him.

Captain Mifflin Kenedy's friendship with Richard King continued even after death parted them. King died the year before Robert Kleberg and Alice King were married, and it was thus Kenedy who gave the bride away in her father's place.[24]

Now Buenos Notches [sic], my little Darling, for I am getting sleepy—and I have a hope that soon my dreams shall lead me to your side. If you will write right now you can address your letter to Corpus Christi. Do not let me wait too long for a letter.

I shall write you when I leave here—Now, my little heart, take good care of yourself & don't have any more headaches & don't work too much on the crazy quilt.

Goodnight. (Kiss)

RJK

Making crazy quilts was a popular pastime in the 1880s, particularly for women of leisure. The fad was inspired by the Japanese asymmetrical art in a popular exhibit at the 1876 Philadelphia Centennial Exposition.[25]

❧

[Addressed to] Miss Alice G. King, Santa Gertrudis, Collins P.O., Nueces Co., Tex. [Written on Stayton & Kleberg stationery.]

Stayton & Kleberg
Attorneys at Law
Victoria, Texas, July 25th, 1884
My Dear Little Heart

You did the proper thing at the proper time when you feared an attack of the blues. You turned your thoughts to me to ward it off. You wrote me a little letter. I hope that it had the desired effect upon you. I can assure you that it was a success as far as I am concerned for it filled my heart with comfort and happiness and caused it to overflow with love for my little [Heart] in the far west. I wish that I could repay you as I feel that you ought to be, but what have I to give as return now? A reassurance that I love you, my little Darling, with all *my heart and all my* soul? *What a meager return for the wealth of such a love as your heart is capable of and which you so unreservedly give to me. I can only justify myself by the thought that* no man *can be fully worthy of your love and that none can give you a truer and more unreserved love than I. This I feel more and more every day, for I learn to know and understand my little sweetheart better all the time. You must not think, my little heart, that I am blind to your faults for if you have any I think I will see them. Doubtless you have them like all who are human, and I expect to see them some time—but that could never change my love—that is one thing in which I pride myself to be perfect in, that is, as full as my nature is capable. I trust my little heart that this item upon which I dwell so much in my letters to you will not grow stale, for I see no relief from you as long as I am permitted to write to you—for I cannot think of you for a moment without such feeling filling every corner of my heart—and driving almost all other thought from my head. And I agree with him who said, "The selfish heart that but by halves is given, Shall have no place in loves delightful heaven."*

Robert was quoting from George Lord Lyttelton's poem "Advice to a Lady" (1781).[26]

You say that you could not in reason look for a letter from me when you wrote. I think you should have and deserve to have a letter whenever you would like to read it, and nothing would give me greater pleasure than to furnish it. This is my excuse for writing again today after having made an attempt to write you day before yesterday, and before I forget it, I want to tell you that you write just as often as you want to—every day—and I think I would enjoy each letter as it came more than the one preceding it.

I am glad you like Mr. Caruthers for he is one of my best friends. Our tastes agree. You may like him as well as I do as a friend—but no better. Do you know that I have always prided myself that I would never feel jealous and that now I know that under certain circumstances I could just be filled with that unholy passion? Yet as long as the perfect faith I have in your affection remains with me I have no fears. The mere thought that I should ever lose this fills my soul with gloom. I shall not speculate on such thoughts again soon.

W. P. Caruthers was one of the three individuals credited with establishing the *Caller* newspaper in Corpus Christi in 1883, with the other primary investors being Eli Merriman and Ed Williams. Richard King was among the original stockholders. Mifflin Kenedy later became a minor stockholder.[27] It is possible that Caruthers, too, was pursuing Alice.

So you had a letter from Miss [Heaney? Henney?]. It seems that my scheme has taken well. Only our evenings apparently in the company with Miss Powell, when Miss [Heaney? Henney?] was not even present, has convinced the "natives" that I am the latest victim. I would be a victim if they were correct in their conclusions. I expect when you hear from the cat hunt that the latest is that [I] have also been victimized by Miss Lovenskiold. I hope all this will not be loves labors lost and that they were thrown off the right tract [sic] *and not torment you any longer with their impertinent inquiries. If that won't do, wait til Miss H comes back this fall—no I will not do that either, for I think too much of her for that, and besides, they may just as well understand now as then that as far as I am concerned that you have all the love that my heart can hold and you alone, and I will pay you for your little sarcasm by coming to Santa Gertrudis oftener than ever if Miss H comes to C.C. And permit me to say "Take occasion to inform you"—that Miss Powell does not resemble you in any manner whatever, the sight of her would never [illegible] use of you unless it be by contrast, but I will describe her to you more fully when I see you. I wonder if Miss [Henning?] volunteered all her information because she thought it would be pleasant for you? How* kind *the people of the world are! What an interest they take in everyone's happiness. I shall certainly put an end to their anxiety on my account, if any they have, at the earliest possible opportunity—*

Robert was being playful and sarcastic about the ladies and their interest in the romance between Robert and Alice. Miss Powell is not identified. Miss Heaney was possibly the daughter of A. G. Heaney.[28]

I have not seen the papers to which you refer but I think the Democratic nomination a very strong one and as far as Cleve-

land is concerned it is as I expected and the nomination for the president is better than I expected for I feared that no man of the prominence of Mr. Hendricks would be satisfied with being placed on the ticket second to Gov. Cleveland. The nomination of Cleveland was made as a bid for the independent Republican vote and for the vote of New York. Yet I doubt whether the nomination is as strong as that of such a man as Bayard would have been, for the Republican's candidate was not chosen with reference to carrying any particular state—but to carry the Republican party generally he was considered as first and is of his party as the rank point of ability and as a statesman; & I think that Bayard holding the same position in the Democratic party would have been their proper leader, then it would have been Greek against Greek. We shall see the results. No one can tell in advance, it is said, for that there are three things that no one can foretell—"the verdict of a petit jury—the result of an election—and whom a woman will marry."

Robert was referring to the Democratic Party's nomination of Grover Cleveland for president. Thomas Hendricks of Indiana, who was nominated unanimously for vice president on the first ballot, was ultimately on the ticket with Cleveland. Thomas F. Bayard was a Democratic senator from Delaware.[29] In 1885, President Grover Cleveland appointed Rudolph Kleberg, Robert's brother, to be US attorney for the Western District of Texas, a position he held until 1889.[30]

I shall comply with your little request but I fear that I will not be able to get a good picture as there is no artist here now but Mr. DePlanque. I shall try him however, and a favor to you that I have kept my promise.

Louis de Planque, who came to be known as Don Luis, was a Brownsville photographer who had started his business in Matamoros before moving to the American side of the river and eventually to Corpus Christi.[31]

I can tell you that I did not attend the Banquet given the delegates here the night of the convention, where wine of course flowed freely and, my little Darling, while I know that your fears on that score are unnecessary and unfounded, I shall ever follow your wishes. First [it] gives me more pleasure to deny drink and please you than to drink, and now I must close for I have "lots" of work to do yet and here I am writing to you, the sweetest token of all. I have written so much foolishness that I cannot read over my letter & I pity you if you accept it.

Robert gave up drinking on most occasions because of Alice's concerns about her father's drinking.[32]

Don't forget now that you are to write just as often as you possibly can & I will do the same. I saw my brother here & learned that my poor Father is still not well, but in no danger nor is he suffering any pain. Direct your letters to me at Meyersville De Witt Co. Tex after you receive this.

Now adios and remember, My little heart, that every Nook and corner of mine is filled with love for you (Kisses) RK

Robert probably saw his brother Rudolph in Victoria, since Rudolph resided in Cuero in DeWitt County, which is adjacent to Victoria County, and Robert's firm had an office in Victoria.

[This letter of August 9, 1884, which no longer has its envelope, was apparently written in Cuero, as Robert wrote that he was "going to start from here by way of Victoria."]

Home Aug 9th 1884
My Dear Little Heart

I have just arrived here again, and found awaiting me two letters from my little Darling—one written in preference to talking to my old rival [McVoy?]—how I wish I could have been in his place that night—how often when this last moon was shedding its glory over the sleeping world have I thought of you and wished that I were with you there for so it is that now there is no place on this wide world, no matter how I have longed to be there when I was away from it or how much I have enjoyed my stay there, but that there have been times when my thoughts turned to you that I have wished that I were with you if but for a few short moments that I might be near you and see you, though perhaps we would have sat in silence as we have so often done, in the past, and I have felt so happy that I did not think to speak except to see your heart open & through your eyes—but I am going to stop this topic if but to take it up again and I am going to answer your letter of the 30th last.

I don't know how it happened that both my letters reached you at the same time though I think I wrote them only a short time apart. I knew that I would not get a letter from you at Victoria—but still I would go on to the post office & hope against hope that perhaps my letters might be forwarded to me there as my stay was so much longer than I had expected when I left home for I intended to be away only for a few days—attending to probate court, but twice when I was ready to start for home I was stopped by parties whom I had to defend in the criminal court. One was a very ridiculous case over a fuss between son-in-law & mother-in-law arising from a crazy quilt. This case I tried making the side of the son-in-law & came out victorious. The other was a very disagreeable case in which there was much feeling against my client. So far I have been successful as this case succeeded in having the same continued until next term of the court when I will be in Corpus or elsewhere & Mr. Stayton & Mr. Crain who is assisting me can fight the fight—

William Henry Crain was a congressman and law partner of Rudolph Kleberg of Cuero and San Antonio.[33]

—but I started to answer your letter first & I am going to do it—so here is the "cat hunt" again—you say that you felt hurt because I did not tell you that I was going—I am sorry that I have caused you pain, my little Darling, but I did not know myself that I was going until the day before, for though I said I would go when I was asked at the time the hunt was first talked of, yet I had no idea at the time that I would participate in this unprecedented amusement. First, because I had no fears that the hunt would actually take place, for I did not think for a moment that the ladies would go, and second I thought I would be away from Corpus at the time set for the hunt & third when I promised to stay over Monday to start out with the cat hunters on next day, I intended to stop with them only for one night—

Now the balance I have told you of in my former letters—so you see the reason why I did not tell you of my going before I left. I have no defense to offer for the propriety of ladies participating in this amusement, and I am not responsible for them—nor am I particularly proud of the part I had in this [illegible] let it be numbered among the things that are past until I see you & then I can tell you many amusing things about it—thus endeth the first chapter—

It appears that Robert participated in a "cat hunt" that particularly distressed Alice since women were present on the hunt. Presumably Robert was hunting for mountain lions (also called pumas or cougars), ocelot, jaguarundi, jaguar, or bobcats. All of these species have been found in the South Texas brush country where Robert was hunting.[34]

Next comes Mr C. of C.C. Well I think you have done the proper thing at the proper time, and I will add, as you ask me for further orders, that you need not enter into any scheme, for the purpose that I did so, for you are not suspected, as far as I know, of giving any grounds for the reasons that are abroad, and more over it would be impossible for you to be as you are and carry on schemes—and have them fully understood by the other par-

ticipants, as at least to the extent, that it was only done for the purpose of seeing how quick madam gossip would take it up. Follow your own good judgment in such matters and you will not be far wrong—Thus endeth the second chapter—

From this passage, it seems that Robert could play these games of misleading the local matrons about romantic interests, but not Alice. Robert's letters continue to suggest that other men were pursuing Alice, and with good reason: the very attractive young woman would inherit considerable land and cash. The mysterious suitor Robert referred to as "Mr. C of C.C." might have been Charles Carroll (see Robert's letter of December 21, 1884, n43 on p. 163). Alternatively, "Mr. C" might have been Robert's good friend W. P. Caruthers, who had earlier visited King Ranch and wrote to Alice. See Robert's letter of July 25, 1884.[35]

But now comes a more serious matter—Mr. Rs. Letter. I can well understand how unpleasant this matter must be to one whose heart is as pure & kind as yours—but I also know that you certainly could not have done anything which intentionally gave any false encouragement to him—that is contrary to your nature. I do not know as only you can know the full import of his letters, but as you have answered him once, he ought to know if he knows you correctly, that it must necessarily give you such pain to be forced to answer him a second time—and I think the best answer you can give him is to remain silent & this will be your best protection for the future. Then your answers will remain the same as contained in your last letter in which you have said all that you could say. I feel more than ever that I should have followed my first impulse in the matter and told your parents at once. No, I won't say that either for I don't know; they have been so kind & good to me that I know since I fear that this matter will cause them trouble, it is perhaps best that they should not see cause at once—but be that as it may we have acted as was thought best for them, and now to the future

I shall embrace at the first opportunity to tell them all & assure them that I will never cause them trouble and that I shall do all in my powers to make their declining days as peaceful & happy as possible, for otherwise you could not feel happy or contented.

Robert's letter indicates that Mr. R (Russell?) had not yet been dissuaded in his pursuit of Alice. The August 31, 1884, issue of the *Corpus Christi Caller* identifies J. C. Russell as the district attorney in Corpus Christi, and it is possible but not ascertainable that he was the mysterious Mr. R. who had written to Alice. Apparently, Robert and Alice had become caught in the web of intrigue that Robert's misleading actions had generated, and it had become necessary for them to confess their true feelings to Alice's parents.

I have never said anything in reply to the little statement contained in your [illegible] letter & certainly appreciate the compliment, and can but confess that it gives me new hopes that I may be able to add happiness to the little circle referred to. I have thought of them so often as my thoughts turned to Santa Gertrudis—and hoped that there [sic] *troubles were lessening, though I feared that this continued drouth would necessarily give your poor father more trouble & worry; and that it would not help your mother's weakness.*

I found my poor father as well as I could hope, for he is still helpless—though his general health is as good as could be expected. My sister has almost entirely recovered, so far all loved ones *prayers have been heard.*

The ill sister could have been either Caroline Eckhardt or Lulu Kleberg, the youngest daughter, who never married. She lived with her parents in Yorktown and took care of them.[36]

Now, my little Darling, Buenos Notches. I am going to start from here next Saturday by way of Victoria, where I will prob-

ably remain for two days & then return to the South to Corpus so that by the end of next week I expect to be in Corpus. I will let you know immediately on my arrival—can't you have a little note there to greet me? With the tenderest devotion, Yours only

(Kiss) [illegible]

❧

[Addressed to] Miss Alice G. King, Collins, Nueces Co., Texas
[posted from Laredo and written on stationery from]
Joseph Christen, Proprietor, Commercial Hotel,
Post Office Lock Box No. 15,
Telephone Connection with all parts of the city. Laredo, Texas

Laredo, Texas

Nov. 13th, 1884

My Dear Little Heart

We reached this glorious place this morning at 5 am, right-side up with care. Capt. Kenedy went with us this far but returned by this morning's train. Your father seems in good spirits and health. He ate a hearty breakfast this morning. I give you particulars because I know how anxious you are about his health. So far our trip has been very pleasant though we had but little sleep during the night.

Robert was in Laredo with Captains Kenedy and King, no doubt on legal matters, possibly related to the railroad.

Well I must close again as our party are ready to start for San Antonio.

On November 17, 1884, a few days after Robert wrote this letter, Richard King was in St. Louis for the National Cattlemen's Association meeting. While there, he and other Texas cattlemen proposed a "National Trail" that would extend from Doan's Crossing on the

Red River north through Indian Territory, the present Oklahoma Panhandle, Colorado, Nebraska, Wyoming, South Dakota, and Montana to the Canadian border. This plan was an attempt to fight the threatened quarantines against Texas cattle and the Texas fever they carried, later found to be caused by ticks.[37]

So good by—will try and drop you a word from San Antonio. Until then adios. May heaven keep and protect my little Darling—

Yours affectionately
Robert J. Kleberg

[Addressed to] Miss Alice G. King, Collins, Nueces Co., Texas

Corpus Christi
Dec. 1st, 1884
My Dear Little Heart

I cannot tell you the happiness your letter gave me to-night. I went to the post office as soon as the mail arrived to get my letter, & on the way I said to myself, if I don't get my letter I will be dreadfully disappointed and if I get it I will almost be afraid to open it for fear that you would persist in your first resolve, but I did not hesitate a moment to open it and read it, for I gathered courage when I thought of the love you had shown me and which I could never doubt or lose faith in, and my faith was richly rewarded by the contents of your letter. I glanced at the end, and there I read in unmistakable words, my own feelings and resolutions. "Yours until death," are no idle words when spoken by you, and I know it and can best understand their full purport when I look in my own heart and find the same words written there. So it shall be and all obstacles that may present themselves will only make those words more indelible, and add redouble[d] force and strength to my resolutions—it is the very essence of my existence and draws nourishment from every fiber and drop of blood in my body. The apparent resistance that has been manifested has only served to prove to me true futility to weaken my love & purpose[.]

Now, my little Darling, perhaps it is because I always look at the bright side of every thing that I do not read your Father's actions as darkly as you do. I know how powerful and impetuous his love for you is. In all his disappointments in his family relations he has looked to you for consolation, and I can well understand with what anxiety he looks upon this all important step of yours. He knows so well that your happiness as well as that of his declining years depend upon it, and he cannot well be too careful. He doubtless feels that he himself is to a great extent responsible for the existing state of circumstances.

Have I not told you how confident I was at first of his approval, and that I gained this confidence from his actions and conversations, which were brought out, no doubt, by my guarded diffident conduct towards you. Has he not talked as kindly and as fatherly towards me as my own father—and spoken to me of the importance which matrimony was in the life of every man? Has he not told me of the beneficent influence which this step had had upon his own life, happiness and success, and with what diffidence and fear he had aspired to win the love of your dear mother, relating to me all the little circumstances of his first courtship—and how he tried to learn and know your mother's real worth and character, by observing her mother, and reasoning that the daughter of such a mother could not well be much unlike her, and then he told me the best way to judge a young lady was by her mother, and then he told me that you were exactly like your mother; all this he has told me after having told me to always consider his house a welcome home, and, that your mother would always bid me welcome, and then closed by telling me that he had never spoken to any one as he had to me—(I do not hesitate, my little Darling, to tell you the innermost thoughts of my heart or I could not tell you all this.) He has not forgotten all this, and perhaps fears that he has encouraged me too much, but he has judged me rightly, for while I had long felt that there was no one whom I held in such high esteem as you, and I felt so grateful to your parents for the many kindnesses they had shown me, how they had invited me into their own warm home and bade me welcome, I certainly struggled with all my force against winning your love, and against betraying my own for you, for fear that I might by so doing prove ungrateful to them and to you that I was asking too much when I craved your love. I say your father judged me rightly. Had I not had every indication that I would always be welcome in your parent's [sic] *house, I should have continued the struggle against my own inclinations longer, & you know and will remember that for a long time I never visited the rancho unless I had business which required it, and when there I did not enter the house except by special invitation—that I, for a long time, I never paid a mere friendly visit except when specially invited, though I had been repeatedly told to come whenever I felt so inclined, that I would always be welcome, and I shall never cease to feel thankful and grateful toward them for these many actions of kindness to me, for I really did not care to visit anywhere else, and how I can forgive any apparent little act of coolness by them toward me, for the [illegible] certainly seem ungrateful that after all their hospitality that I should ask for that which they prize more than everything else on this earth, their* "little pets" *love, all that was left in their home to shed sunshine upon it—and Heaven forbid that I ever do anything that would give them reason to regret that they had been so hospitable and kind to me. No it shall be my life's task to prove to them that they have not placed their kindness upon an ungrateful, an unworthy one—And I can but think that the time is not far distant when they will know me well enough for this. For by the love I have for you which is stronger than all other passions that move within me, I shall never cease to try and prove worthy of their highest respect and esteem—and I can truly say that my esteem and friendship for them has not grown any less because of their apparent reluctance to give their consent to our union—and while we will never be united without their consent—still there is nothing on this earth to which I would yield of our love. This I must retain—come what may and as long as I have that I shall never grow weary to endeavor to win their consent, and to prove to them that I am not unworthy of the high trust they have placed upon me.*

Now, my Little Darling, I have written perhaps more earnestly than usual, but I hope I have said nothing that will give you pain or trouble—for your kind letter deserves a better answer. I think you will look for this tomorrow and you shall not be disappointed, and I will try and be as good as I know how and am able.

Captain King had not at this point given approval for the marriage of Alice and Robert to take place. Richard King's disappointments in family relations would have included the marriage of his daughter Nettie on November 23, 1878, to Major E. B. Atwood, an army officer and a "Yankee."[38] Richard King was an avowed Confederate, with a son named for Robert E. Lee, so it may have been a cruel blow to have a US Army officer in the family. It had been only eleven years since Union soldiers hunting for King had raided the rancho. The troops had destroyed the furnishings, commandeered livestock and some workers, killed one Kineño, and held the family captive for a while. After the troops released the family, they immediately fled, all while Henrietta was pregnant with their son Lee. The family and Captain King lived as fugitives until the end of the war.[39]

Ella King's marriage to Louis M. Welton was apparently troubled from the beginning. Baby Etta arrived only seven months after the wedding, and Ella continued to experience unhappiness and distress.[40]

I wish other people would attend to their own affairs and let us attend to ours. I hope that the long expected guests will come soon if they are coming at all—for I should like to assist your father in entertaining them when they come—and after the 8th of this month I will have [to] be in court and attendance upon our court. Now good night, my own true heart, may heaven bless and protect you—and yours—with sincere prayer of your affectionate lover—

Robert Kleberg

❧

[Addressed to] Miss Alice G. King, Collins, Nueces Co., Tex.

R. W. Stayton, Victoria R. J. Kleberg, Corpus Christi
Law Office
Stayton & Kleberg
Victoria and Corpus Christi, Texas
Corpus Christi, Dec. 11, 1884
My Dear Little Heart,

Your more than welcome letter reached me night before last, and I assure you it caused no frowns but filled my heart with peace and happiness. Perhaps if I consumed the day time in writing to you, tonight it might be said that I devoted that time to something else. It would be better, but I have been at work all day and a good part of the night in answer[ing] letters. Now all are ready to retire except those who are dancing just across the street and I certainly have this time for myself and I am using it to the best purpose in the world—when I am writing to my Little Darling and I know too that her letters do not keep me from doing my duty, but on the contrary are the greatest encouragement to me to do my duty to the fullest extent, and they keep me from spending any time perhaps at the dance across the street from my office—and then I would not be as well fitted for court as I will be now, for as soon as I finish this I shall seek the healing balm of natures sweet rest over.

I saw your father and mother every evening except the first evening they were here. In fact, I spent most of the evenings with them. They were both as cordial and kind towards me as they could be, which I was with them. They both seemed very well after the first evening.

I saw your friend and mine Miss M[?] across the way this evening. She smiled, bowed as sweetly as could be. Let them all talk and try to estrange my heart from you as much as they will, but there is no earthly power that can change my love for you except you. As long as I have your love I am armed against them all. Let them use what weapons they will.

Now I must close for my light has burned up all the oil. This is a shorter letter than you deserve, but remember, my little Darling, that though my letter may not be so long in extension, my love for you is constantly growing—deeper and deeper & warmer and that I send Y. W. D. W. D. P. [?] Robert J. Kleberg

❧

[Addressed to] Miss Alice G. King, Collins, Nueces Co. Texas

MYRTLE CLUB
Dec. 21, 1884

Your little letter of the 19th did not want to be taken out of the post office last [night], and after reading over only the first page I at once admitted the force of the point you made and its unanswerable argument in support of the same and here I am ready to abide [by] your judgment.

I moved yesterday into my new quarters and in consequence [I] have to resort to the stationary [sic] *of the Myrtle Club—as everything is in a sweet state of confusion both in my room and in my office—so you will pardon the heading to*

> *this paper over the place I have chosen for a few words with my Little Darling—all alone here in our club rooms—where everything is as quiet as the [illegible] to be[?].*

According to the *Corpus Christi Caller* of December 28, 1884, "Capt. DeRyee has removed his family over his drug store and the bachelors Kleberg, McGregor, and Lackey now roost at Charley's late residence."[41] The Myrtle Club, founded in 1883 and named after a cigar that was popular at the time, was probably the first social club established in Corpus Christi.[42] The all-male membership gathered upstairs over the Doddridge Bank to study literature, read newspapers and magazines in the reading room, and play billiards and cards in the game room.[43] The *Corpus Christi Caller* reported on April 27, 1884, that the "Myrtle Club is flourishing. Going to raise dues from 15- to $25—advise those contemplating joining to put in their application."

> *I am sorry to hear that you have been so unwell and hope that you have entirely recovered by this time. I heard of the arrival of Richard III as nice Xmas present for the Puerta—and I can well imagine how proud Richard King II is and I trust that the Young King may fill the aching void in the hearts of your good parents. I long to meet the young man myself and to see the happy smile of his Little Mother. I must unto to Richard today.*

Richard King III was born December 17, 1884.[44] The December 21, 1884, issue of the *Corpus Christi Caller* announced the birth: "Mr. Richard King Jr., [*sic*] is the happy father of a bouncing baby boy. Richard the Third Has Arrived."

> *I can hardly await the time when Xmas will come. Never since the days of my early boyhood has the time seemed to drag along so slowly just before Xmas, and never have I looked forward to Xmas even with more pleasure than now when I shall be with my own true Little Heart.*

Now I must stop my letter talk for here come my friends Mrs. [Gostessy?] and Mr. [Keenan?] whom I have promised to take to church. Now it is time for us to go. So now goodby for the present.

If I was prepared to write in my room I would write more tonight for I always like to have a chat with my little darling when "coursed sun is en rapt in sleep: and silence reigns supreme," but this time I fear I will not have that pleasure, so now again goodby until I see you next week. Be careful of your health and when we meet, our ecstacy [sic] *will be so sweet, my Little Darling, that it will make up for the many hours of bitter separation.*

Goodby—kiss mmmmmmmmmmmmmmmmmmm

Yours U D U D P RJK

Apparently Robert and Alice had developed a code that they used occasionally in their letters. The ending of this letter is an example of that.

My Little Darling

[Addressed to] Miss Alice G. King, Santa Gertrudis, Collins, Texas Thursday 1 AM

Corpus Christi

January 1st 1885

My Dear Little Heart—

If I were not afraid that illness was the cause of my not hearing from you tonight I would scold you terribly. I have felt so disappointed at not getting a word from you by tonight's mail that I hardly knew what to do. First I said well I don't feel like writing to her now so I betook myself to reading a book. The title is Alice, and I read until the old year had silently passed into the ocean of eternity.

Then I quit reading and sat by the fire and listened to the mournful requiem of the norther over the [cow?] pens. Then I looked out on the bay where the boats were tossing over the rough waters. No comfort in all that. I finally turn again to My Little Heart—for I know I can't sleep until I wish her a happy New Year and perhaps (?) she is looking for a word from me today, and I will not disappoint her for I feel too keenly how I miss that greeting myself. But I was not going to grumble any more. I know it is not your fault, my little Darling.

I left your father and mother this evening about 7½ to take my supper and from there to the mail *and from there to the Presbyterian Sunday School Xmas tree. It was a success from all appearances, for the little children seemed happy over their presents. Your father & mother as well as usual.*

Again a happy New Year. Now good night, my Little Heart! (Kisses) Yours RJK

The Presbyterian church was apparently celebrating a version of the Twelve Days of Christmas, with the First Day being December 26. Robert was writing this letter on January 1, which would have been the Seventh Day of Christmas. January 6, celebrated in some religious traditions as Epiphany, is the Twelfth Day of Christmas.

❧

[The envelope for this letter from W. P. Caruthers is missing.]

Corpus Christi
March 29, 1885
Sunday
Miss King:

Of all the compliments passed on the Collins Exposition number that have come to me through the press by letter or by word of mouth, there is not one that I appreciate as highly as the few words from you. I feel sure you would not pay me a false compliment, for there is no cause for it; and I don't believe you deal in flattery at any time. I give you credit for sincerity. And I know you are fully competent in every way to pass judgment on the merits and demerits of such a production. So few persons are. Please believe that I would not attempt to flatter you

There is so much of adverse criticism and so little that is cheering in the life of a journalist that kind words and good wishes expressed by one whom he has every reason to hold in the highest esteem, come like rays of sunshine out of the cloudy, wintry sky. Could I have carried out all my plans in producing the illustrated number it would have been more worthy of your good words. I thank you.

I learn with sincere regret that your father's health is not improving as rapidly as it should. I esteem him as one of my best friends, and I appreciate the favors he has done me. Therefore, if it is now within my power to help him I will gladly do it. Do you not need some one to sit up with him? Can I be of any service? If so, let me know and I will go to San Antonio and do all I can. I presume you are dependent more or less on strangers. I have some business there and can go at any time. So if you should need any one remember I will respond promptly to a call. I hope your father will soon be well.

Remember me kindly to your parents and accept for yourself my best wishes and again my thanks for your generous words.

Very sincerely,
W. P. Carruthers

Caruthers evidently had written an article about the Collins Exposition for his newspaper. Caruthers, who was one of Robert's best friends and also a friend of Captain King, was possibly also pursuing Alice, particularly in her time of need.

Robert and Alice had been going through a difficult time because her parents had apparently not consented to their marriage. After four years of courtship with Alice, Robert had written to Henrietta King, in the Victorian manner, on October 12, 1884, and requested Alice's hand in marriage.[45] According to one source, the betrothal was announced with no definite date for the wedding but that the couple received congratulations from family members and friends.[46] However, Robert's earlier letter of December 1, 1884, casts serious doubt that the engagement had been made public. It certainly indicated that Captain King was having second thoughts about allowing his "Pet" and dutiful daughter Alice to marry and leave his home. Both Captain King and Henrietta had come to rely heavily on Alice to take care of the rancho and Captain King during Henrietta's frequent absences.

Robert's letter of December 1 also reaffirmed their devotion to each other "until death." He certainly left no doubt that he would wait as long as was necessary and would never marry without the consent of Alice's parents. Captain King's lukewarm reaction to the engagement apparently surprised Robert because he had seemed confident of the captain's positive feelings toward him; now that the engagement had been proposed, Captain King seemed to be blaming himself for letting the couple's relationship develop to this point. It may be it was the father-in-law who was getting cold feet and not the groom. This turn of events certainly appeared to have the "gossips" intrigued, and both Alice and Robert seemed tired of hiding their relationship and of the public gossip about their private lives.

The captain and Henrietta were pleased with Robert's courtship but perhaps were not ready to give their daughter in marriage in the near future. The fact that Robert was welcomed at Christmas indicates that Captain King was still glad to have Robert in his home. It is curious, though, that on New Year's Eve Captain and Mrs. King were in Corpus Christi and visiting with Robert but Alice remained at home.

There may have been another good reason why Captain King was reluctant at this time to give his consent for Robert to marry Alice. Captain King's battle with stomach cancer was fast coming to an end. Shortly after Robert's letter of January 1, 1885, on January 4, the *Corpus Christi Caller* reported that "Captain King had taken quite sick in this city but on Saturday was better." Then on January 18 it was reported that "a special train left this city last Wed. morning for Collins, having as passengers Capt. R. King and wife, Wm Chamberlain, R. Holbein and Dr. T. S. Burke. The Captain was much better from his recent illness and is hoped still rapidly improving." It is interesting that Captain King did not use a special train car but instead had his own special train to take him back to Santa Gertrudis and that he was accompanied by a physician, Dr. Burke. Even though the captain was apparently in a great deal of pain, it still took Alice and Henrietta more than a month to persuade him to travel to San Antonio and place himself under a doctor's care there.[47]

During the time between mid-January, when Captain King returned to the rancho from Corpus Christi, and February 25, when he left for San Antonio, the family worked to get their business in order. It may well have been during this time that Captain King, Henrietta, and Alice reached the understanding that he did indeed give his blessing to Robert and Alice's marriage but that he did not want it to be soon. He may have discussed with Henrietta that he wanted Robert to assist her in handling not only his estate but also the rancho.

On February 25, 1885, Captain King left Rancho Santa Gertrudis for the last time. He asked Reuben Holbein, the manager of King Ranch, to write a letter to his lawyer Jim Wells at Brownsville to "tell him to keep on buying" and to "tell him, tell him not to let a foot of dear old Santa Gertrudis get away from us."[48] Shortly after arriving in San Antonio, Dr. Ferdinand Herff, the same doctor who had treated Petra Kenedy, told the captain that his stomach cancer was at the terminal stage. Henrietta finally persuaded her husband to stop drinking in hopes of prolonging his life.[49]

In the meantime, Captain King and the family received the news that on March 19 their beloved friend Mifflin Kenedy had lost his wife to cancer in Corpus Christi. They immediately wrote their condolences to Captain Kenedy, and on March 26 Kenedy wrote to Henrietta at the Menger Hotel in San Antonio to say that their letter had been received.[50] Kenedy also sent news of Robert, who had left for Brownsville that morning to look into business matters.[51] Robert was thus still busy taking good care of both men and their business interests.

[Addressed to] Miss Alice G. King, Menger Hotel, San Antonio, Tex.

Brownsville 4/1 [1885]
Wednesday
My Dear Little heart—

Many thanks for your more than welcome letter of the 26th. It was the first letter handed through the delivery this evening, as I was on hand and just as confident of getting a letter as any body could be. Yes, my little Darling, I was at your good old house when you wrote your last letter and while the place did not have its usual attractions still I too must confess that I have a strong attachment for the place. For there is no place outside of my own good old house, & which I do not expect to see very often again, that is more like a home to me than Santa Gertrudis.

Ah, my little Darling, I cannot tell you how my heart was filled with sadness at the cheerless news from your poor father & yet it gives me relief to know that it lightens the weight of your grief to unburden your heart to me. It is in such trials that we feel the value of true friendship and love and the sympathy of those who love us, and this, my Little Heart, you know you have to the fullest extent from me and while the prospect of your dear father's recovery does not seem to brighten much, still there is an old saying that even while there is life there is hope. Much less should we grow despondent now for there are so many cases that have baffled the learning of the most skilled & learned men & yet nature in her mysterious way has worked a complete cure & so I have strong hopes that before long your father's iron constitution and his unconquerable will will win the fight and force themselves from the sneeking [sic] *clutches of diseases. Do not think, my little Darling, that your account of your father's sickness grew wearisome to me for there is nothing more interesting to me. Do I not know that there is nothing that so fills your mind and heart as that? Everybody that meets me inquires anxiously about your father's health & express their sympathy for him on account of this long suffering and express an earnest wish that he may soon recover.*

I can't tell yet when I'll [illegible] through here. I intend to stay until I have done all that I can do. So far I have gotten along very well & I do not anticipate much trouble for there I was received when I had left my own house as by a new home and I have always considered it the greatest compliment your father ever paid me when he told me to consider the place as my home, that I was always welcome there, and every place that greets my eyes there is connected with some pleasant memory. There I found a little Heart that has given new life and light to my [whole?] being. How often have I felt when I was away from that dear old place that while the world might elsewhere present a thousand and one beauties of nature and art that were not to be found there, still of all the world, that was the place that I would have preferred going to & where I heard others speak of all other interesting places in the world that they would prefer going to. I thought that my wishes were more modest perhaps, but let me go to Santa Gertrudis & let others to—to where they pleased. Yet on my last visit I fully recognized that there was that wanting in the place that threw such a chasm about the place for me. I did not here [sic] *the footsteps that I learned to know so well passing my room in the morning before going to breakfast, the sound of which made my heart beat faster &*

filled it with a strange and wonderful rapture that I could no longer sleep but I felt like rising (not because I wanted breakfast) but I wanted to hear a low sweet voice bid me "good morning," and I longed to catch one short glance from a pair of dark eyes.

So you won't trust me now to say whether I would like to take you with me as my wife? Let me tell you, little tormentor, I will always be so glad to have you with me on my trips as I would have been to have had you with me on this one. You will not often be left if you wish to accompany me.

Imagine my disappointment when I found after my arrival here that my old friend Mr. Cocke was not here. She is visiting her parents in Cuero & will not return while I am here. Don't you sympathize with me?

In 1884, J. J. Cocke was the county surveyer in Cameron County; Henrietta owed him money after Richard King's death.[52] J. J. Cocke was also a visitor documented as having stayed at Los Laureles when Mifflin and Petra Kenedy owned that rancho.[53] Robert was apparently being sarcastic about his "disappointment" at missing Mr. and Mrs. Cocke.

It is a good thing your letter arrived this evening before I went over into Matamoros & saw the dark warm lights of the señorita's eyes, and let me assure you, my Little Heart, that it is utterly impossible for me to think of loving anyone but you. Such a thought or possibility of such a thing never would have entered my thoughts had you not spoken of it. That is out of the question. My heart is at rest in your love. It cares for no other & will have no other. That is a fixed fact. Just as much so as that there is no one else who can ever wear the love that I feel for my own mother. *No one can take her place & no one can take your place in my heart, for that love has become a part of my very nature and you need not fear that the fountain of that love will ever cease to flow for you. No one else can drink there but you, and the more you drink it, the clearer and sweeter, stronger will flow the current of that love, for it always seems to me the more I try to let it overflow the more I feel my incapability of exhausting it. It is like a hole. The more you take from it the larger it grows. Not a very poetic comparison but it illustrates the thought.*

Robert and Alice have developed a playful, coquettish relationship, with a strand of jealousy running through it. She has sent him a love poem, and he is responding with poetic prose.

You once told me that I was conceited. Do you remember? (No, you don't.) Let me warn you if you apply such pictures of a man as is given by the little piece of poetry you enclose to me, I will grow conceited.

Now, good night, my little heart, & remember that when we meet, our spirits shall mesh together as we drink at its same fountain, and we shall feel that bliss that is the sweet reward of true love.

I will read the sermon you sent me tonight. I will probably wire before I leave here, to your father when I leave, so you can know when I will leave.

The sermon to which Robert referred was probably one by the Reverend John W. Neil, pastor of the First Presbyterian Church in San Antonio. Henrietta and Alice likely attended the church because the Reverend Neil was a friend.

Now may Heaven be with you, my Little Heart, and hear your prayers. Good night (Kiss) Yours always, Robert

The day after Robert wrote to Alice from Brownsville on April 1, 1885, Captain King wrote out his will in San Antonio. Mifflin Kenedy had traveled to San Antonio to sit by his lifelong friend's bedside as he made out his will and to comfort the family, even as he grieved the recent death of his wife, Petra. All of the other King family members were present except for Nettie King Atwood and her husband, who was ill.[54] According to the *Brownsville Times,* Robert was expected to stay in Brownsville the week of April 5, and we know from his letter to Alice on April 1 that he was writing from Brownsville, so he could not have drawn up Captain King's will in San Antonio, as earlier reported.[55] King's will, executed on April 2, was witnessed by Jacob Waelder and Uriah Lott and named Mifflin Kenedy, Perry Doddridge, and Henrietta as executors of the estate. The *Corpus Christi Caller* reported on April 5 that Captain Kenedy and Perry Doddridge had left for San Antonio on a special train the previous Sunday night, which would have put them there for the drawing of the will. The newspaper also speculated on rumors, one being that they had been called to the bedside of Captain King and the other, that they undertook their journey in order to confer with the directors of the San Antonio and Aransas Pass Railway about extending the route to the port of Corpus Christi.

Sometime between April 1 and April 15 Robert was able to get to San Antonio and be by Alice's side as Captain King grew weaker and weaker. On April 12 the *Corpus Christi Caller* reported sad news about Captain King from the *San Antonio Express,* which said that "the eminent physicians who were called to consult with Dr. Herff pronounced his malady a hopeless and incurable one though everything that science can accomplish will be utilized to prolong the life of the sufferer." The Corpus Christi newspaper also reported receiving private telegrams that corroborated the sad tidings. On April 14, as dusk fell across the Alamo city, Captain Richard King passed from this world.

Captain King had helped tame the Wild Horse Desert and set in motion the western expansion of the United States to the Pacific. He had developed barren land by promoting the expansion of the railroads. With a few scraggly longhorn cattle and the knowledge and expertise of the Kineños, he had created a cattle empire and a family dynasty. He had the toughness it took to settle the land and the business sense to make it successful. He had been a simple man with driving ambition and a fierce love for his family and his land.

The day after his death his funeral was held in the parlors of the Menger Hotel at four-thirty in the afternoon. Reverend J. W. Neil officiated at the services. Large throngs of prominent people who were friends of the deceased filled the parlors and corridors. The most elegant casket that could be procured was decorated with white flowers and surrounded by floral tributes from friends.[56]

After the funeral the family and close friends, including Robert, remained in San Antonio to take care of details, and then they traveled back to Santa Gertrudis. Robert and Captain Kenedy accompanied the family back to the rancho and returned to Corpus Christi the next day.[57] The ranch house must have seemed very quiet and lonely without the captain. Wasting no time, Henrietta appointed Robert to be the new ranch manager and to do as the captain had hoped, "as I myself might do were I living."[58]

The next months for Robert were very busy as he not only took on the role of ranch manager but also supported both Alice and Henrietta in their grief and helped them with their personal business matters. He also had his legal work to deal with, which kept him moving around the state. As the new manager of the rancho, he found that King's estate had $564,784 worth of real estate and $496,700 worth of livestock and other property, making the estate worth a total of $1,061,484. On the other hand, King had left $500,000 in debts that had to be addressed immediately. Captain Kenedy and Perry Doddridge decided that Henrietta, with Robert's help, could manage her affairs, so they declined to act as executors of the estate, thus leaving Henrietta in total control.[59] Robert moved to have Henrietta assume the indebtedness of the rancho, and within ten years they had cleared all of the debts.[60]

Henrietta also took charge of the family's gravesites. The *Corpus Christi Caller* reported on June 14 that they had learned from the *San Antonio Express* that the King monument in St. Louis had been transferred to San Antonio; this was certainly the monument that had been erected for Lee when he died there in 1883. The *Caller* article quoted the San Antonio newspaper's report that "the beautiful and exquisite monument which had been erected in the family burying grounds at St. Louis arrived in three cars yesterday—It is 27 feet high made of a very beautiful and fine quality granite from Hurricane Island, Md. Surmounted by a delicately wrought urn and other carvings lower down on the shaft. The large lot in the cemetery 25x62 ft. will be handsomely enclosed with granite coping, altogether forming one of the finest monuments in the State of Texas."

[Addressed to] Miss Alice G. King Santa Gertrudis,
Collins, Nueces Co. Tex

Laredo May 8th 1885
My Dear Little Heart

Here I am again in this heroic city—my fears were [illegible] and well founded.

*All night long the rain fell, at any rate from the time that I wrote until after twelve, I heard the rain dashing against the window of my room. I was so tired I could not sleep though I went to bed immediately after having written my note to you. I picked up my book—*The Colonels Daughter*—& read and then I tried to sleep but I could not for I thought of a little daughter on the Santa Gertrudis & of the last moments I had spent with her, & how I wished I could be with her there again.*

Robert was probably reading *The Colonel's Daughter, or, Winning His Spurs,* by General Charles King (no relation to Captain King), a very popular novelist of the time and a military man by training. He wrote more than sixty books, as well as numerous articles and short stories, many of them based on his own experiences in serving in the West. They are "exciting narratives full of accurate, detailed descriptions of army life and Indian wars in the American West."[61]

> *I turned to my book until my eyes began to burn & then I quit for I knew that little daughter would not like it & then I fell to sleep and several times a little frisky pony scampered through my dreams—sometimes his name was Ranger and then it was something else & I finally was back riding horseback through Lovers Lane with the dearest companion to me on earth & then such a peaceful refreshing sleep—filled with little short dreams that carried me about from place to place & then finally landed me near a window in which someone was sitting & then I dreamed I tried to put a ring on my finger but my finger was too clumsy. Then I began to pay for my ring but the more I paid the more I felt I owed—but such a sweet debt. The longer it grew the happier it made me. I felt that I wanted to keep paying it off & still I did not want it [illegible] my little darling. This debt & the desire to pay off constitutes the mainspring to my whole life.*
>
> *I can't thank you enough for your little present. I did not know that [I] could appreciate it as much as I do. A long time ago you gave me a little present, just before I left for this place. I had it in my vest pocket & when in my room here—the same I am occupying now—I took it from my pocket and began thinking of the giver—and when I put it to my lips—not to kiss it then—but to blow it, it made very strange music. I thought again of the giver & wondered if it had been given with any motive in meaning. Yes I deserved it. I had made a goose of myself. That was it & this little present would assist me in speaking in my mother tongue. Do you remember the little duck caller you gave me? But now I have yet another present to play with. I try in vain to place it on my finger & wondered if you would object to my having it enlarged so that I could wear it?*

Alice had previously given Robert a duck call as a gift, and her most recent gift to him was apparently a ring that Robert needed to get resized before he could wear it. This letter clearly shows their shared sense of humor.

I stopped here, as the train was just about to start [at?] 5 P.M. arriving San Antonio May 9th 6 A.M. I arrived here at 3½ A.M. & start now for Austin. Train was delayed by washouts. Goodby (Kiss) Your Robt.

❧

[This letter is addressed to Alice at 3815 Delmar Avenue, St. Louis, Missouri.]

Robert had spent much of the summer helping Henrietta and supporting Alice. After settling her personal and business matters in Texas, Henrietta traveled to St. Louis on August 16, to visit daughter Ella King Welton, and Alice accompanied her.

Corpus Christi Aug 21/85
My Dear Little Heart
I received your letter of Sunday evening last night but did not find time to answer it as I had an engagement with Capt. Kenedy and the old gentleman generally has a great deal to talk about and so I did not leave him until nearly twelve & when I got downtown I met Mr. Wells who had an interminable long talk about business, the result of all of which was that I failed to write to your mother on yesterday as I had fully intended.

Robert's talk with James B. Wells would probably have been about land grant claims, as that was one of his specialties, learned from his late partner Stephen Powers. Wells had entered the University of Virginia law school in 1874 and received his degree one year later. Robert Kleberg had also attended the University of Virginia law school, in 1879, so although the two were not classmates, they had an alma mater in common.[62] Wells also had an unofficial connection to Powers, having married his niece, Pauline Kleiber, on November 4, 1880.[63]

> *Today I have been unusually busy attending to business for Capt. Kenedy. I felt quite complimented that he should entrust the matter to me, the more, as he had concluded to take my advice on the matter given him some time ago.*

Mifflin Kenedy began settling his wife Petra's estate in August 1885 after her death on March 15. She had died intestate "because it would have been expensive to go through the courts, and a division of the property would have been bad for him. He settled with each of the children—both Petra's with Luis Vidal and Petra's with him—for $50,000 for their interest in Petra's estate, with either promissory notes or deeds to land and real estate. He had no cash settlements. Intestate law said that the surviving spouse received one-half of the deceased's half of the community property, and the children split the other half equally. Mifflin would be doling out $350,000 in promissory notes and/or deeds to land and real estate, which made Petra's total estate worth $700,000."[64] Robert would have had much to do with helping Kenedy handle the situation. Petra's surviving children with Luis Vidal were Luisa, Concepción, María Vicenta, and Rosa. The surviving children with Mifflin were Tom, John, and Sarah. Petra and Mifflin's grandson George, the child of their late son James, inherited when Mifflin died. Petra and Luis's granddaughter Anita, the child of Adrián Vidal, who died in 1865, also inherited later on.[65]

> *That together with a thousand and one things has kept me harder at work than usual. The fact is that I have not only failed to find time for a* siesta *in the afternoon but I hardly get enough sleep at night and you know how I enjoy it even more here, away from you than when I am near you, for do you know, my little Heart, I dream as soon as I fall to sleep, and there my little*

Mifflin Kenedy and his grandchildren Sarah, Georgie, and John Jr. Mifflin Kenedy was very close to Robert and Alice Kleberg. At their wedding, he stood in for Alice's father—his late friend, Richard King—and Robert and Alice later named their first child Richard Mifflin Kleberg.

Darling is brought to my side, and we have such happy little talks in the hammock in the hall at home—or on the cars on the way to St. Louis. For the good angel that watches over me when I lay me down to sleep knows that I never sleep so sweetly as when in my dreams you are near me and for that reason he leads me across hills and vales & streams & forests & prairies on the swift railway train.

I am glad that your mother stood the trip so well. Tell me do you eat meat? and sleep enough? Do try to and you will soon be strong. I told you often that your gloomy imagination caused you much unnecessary worry.

So you found your little niece as well and happy as could be. When I first read of the grand reception you met at the depot I began to feel badly that I could not be there. I thought you had reference to your friends & I felt relieved that it was [Maxwell?] they came to see. That's a nice compliment is it not?

Robert was referring to Alice's niece Etta, daughter of Ella King Welton in St. Louis. Etta was a great favorite of her grandmother, Henrietta.

But the fact is I don't care if your St. Louis admirers make themselves scarce. I don't want them to bask in my little Pet's smiles. I prefer that you should look at the little engraving you spoke of in your letter and then you may smile and think of the pleasant, the happy moments that we have spent together.

The "little engraving" may be a portrait of him by Louis de Planque, about which he wrote in his letter of July 25, 1884.

I do not know of any other moments than happy that have passed where we were together. Even in the saddest moments, our being together gave us all the relief that we could find on earth from our cares and sorrows. For it is but too true that in our gloomiest moments we learn to love each other most and we can appreciate best the sweet consolation of love's sympathy. Oh, my own true Little Heart, how can I tell you the happiness and peace that fills my heart and mind at the thought of being able someday of clasping you in my arms as my little wife. It seems to me that I would never want to let you loose again. How that last sweet kiss at parting makes me yearn for the first kiss of our meeting. How your last linger[ing] look makes me look forward to the first glance of those dear loving eyes when they first meet mine on your return.

I am not showing good manners to my guest Mr. Robt. Stayton. My good friend & partner came over to pay me a visit and is sitting near me reading, waiting for me to get through with my long letter writing. He is trying to get me to go with him tomorrow evening across the bay to see his little boy & wife & I would like the best in the world to get off tomorrow evening & return the next evening. It is only twelve miles to Ingleside where they are & he says that it is a shame that I have not paid him a visit in all this time that they have been so near.

Now good night, my own true Little Alice. May heaven protect you and your good mother. Give her my love & tell her that surely tomorrow will be her time for a letter. You may read it over her shoulder.

As the new manager of King Ranch, Robert was writing to Henrietta about ranch business.

Now again, good night—(Kisssssss) from your
Robert

❧

[Addressed originally to Miss Alice G. King, 3815 Delmar Avenue, St. Louis, Missouri; that address was scratched out and replaced with an address to Robt. J. Kleberg, Corpus Christi, Nueces Co., Tex.]

Alice apparently had left St. Louis before the letter arrived, so it was returned to Robert.

> *Corpus Christi Aug. 24th/85*
> *My Dear Little Heart*
> *I have been hard at work all day drawing up legal documents for Capt. Kenedy, & now that all may be well that ends well I shall at the close of the day write to you, my own precious darling, for after supper I have an engagement with Capt. Kenedy & I know it will be late before I will get through there.*
>
> *Just think of it. [It] is over eight days since you wrote the last letter which I received (you wrote last Sunday). It seems twice that long. I thought yesterday evening on my return to the city from Ingleside where I went last Saturday evening to visit my friend Robt. Stayton & see his wife & boy, that I would find a letter. I went directly from the wharf, where the boat landed that brought me across the bay, to the post office but only business letters & a law journal greeted me there. Well tonight I am sure I will hear from my little pet. I cannot tell you with what anxiety I am awaiting to hear how your trip & visit is benefiting you and your mother.*
>
> *I am afraid that I wrote her too long a letter about business matters but I could not well avoid it. Besides, if she did not hear from me often she might imagine that all was not going right and that would worry her more than the little business worry.*
>
> *I had quite a pleasant little visit at Ingleside. Mr. Stayton came over for me in a buggy, but I could not leave here until after 4 P.M. & it is 18 miles from here & across the reef which you cannot cross in much less time than an hour. So we did not reach the end of our trip until after sundown, but it was a bright moonlight night and we had a very pleasant drive in.*

Ingleside is on Corpus Christi Bay at the eastern tip of San Patricio County.[66]

On our arrival we found other visitors there—Mr. Geo. Fulton, wife & two young ladies from Rockport.

George Ware Fulton Jr., rancher and attorney, settled in Rockport in 1879 to be near his parents and those of his wife, Leonora Caruthers. Fulton practiced law in Rockport, mainly taking care of legal affairs for the Coleman-Fulton Pasture Company.[67]

I spent the evening playing with the boy who seemed to take to me wonderfully having heard so much about me. I had not seen him for over a year. He is a fine boy, 28 months old. The young ladies entertained us with songs so the time passed well enough. I remained next day until 5 P.M. when I took a boat across the bay to Corpus & in a short time, less than two hours, I was in Corpus. Had full sail across the bay, which was just rough enough to make it lively. How I wish my little Heart could have been with me on the boat. You would have enjoyed it, I know, for I do not think a sailboat would make you sick.

Mr. Stayton leaves for his house in Victoria today. I wish I could make the trip with him & then go home from there but our court is still in session & as the special judge has failed to put in an appearance this week I fear that I will be detained here all next week & then the week after that I have a case in Rockport. But I will not fill your letter with all the disagreeable things I am looking forward to. There is one consolation. I will get through with all the work as well as I can so that I will have more time to be with you, my Little Darling, when you return; I have had the good luck not to meet Mrs. S. so far & I hear she intends leaving in the morning to be away for some time, so her father informed us. Where to I did not ask. So I am getting on finely in that respect. I had feared that as she was so persistent when I was in town last before this that she would continue, but it seems that she has probably learned better sense since then.

Robert's mention of "Mrs. S." was a reference to Sarah Spohn, Mifflin Kenedy's daughter, who seemed intent on discovering the relationship between Robert and Alice.

> *I did not hear from Santa Gertrudis since I saw Mr. Doughty last Saturday. I had hoped that I would find time to make a flying trip over there some time this week to see how things were coming on, but I fear now from the way business is pressing here that I will not be able to go.*

Mr. James M. Doughty was the foreman at King Ranch. His son A. C. "Mack" Doughty handled the infrastructure around headquarters.[68] Robert's schedule was full because he was acting manager of the rancho and was also handling its legal affairs as well as those of many other clients.

> *Now I am going to bid you good evening until 8 P.M. when I will have a little quiet time reading your letter and then I will let my thoughts turn to all the many happy little moments we have spent together & then I will call on old Capt. Kenedy. Poor old man, he is worrying considerably about fixing up his business matters with his children & wife's children. I hope they will behave themselves.*

Robert was still working on Captain Kenedy's estate planning.[69] By this time, Robert and Captain Kenedy had grown very close to each other.

> *Now again, good evening. The supper bell is calling me to my supper.*
>
> *Last night, darling, after writing your mother I was terribly hungry when I got to my room, so I looked in my ginger snap box & sure enough I found a half a dozen snaps, just as nice as*

they could be, but now they are out, so hurry & come back that you keep me from starving physically and mentally.

Besides sending Robert little gifts like the duck call mentioned previously, Alice also baked cookies for him to take home.

I am getting terribly hungry to see my little Darling, to clasp her in my arms and to look in those dark eyes where I read what words cannot speak & there I would answer with a (kiss) Adios. Yours with oceans of love, and yours only, Robert.

My regards to your mother.

[Sent to] Miss Alice G. King, 3815 Delman Avenue, St. Louis, Mo.
15 W. Missouri Avenue Kansas City Missouri.
[Edwin E. Wilson is at the top of the envelope.]

Friday Corpus Christi Sept. 4, 1885

My Dear Little Heart,

I shall never forget the first time I wrote those words and how happy I was that I could tell you what you were to me, My dear little heart. Nor have these words lost any of their magic charm since then for me. It always gives me relief and fills my soul with peace and happiness beyond all measure when I know that I can rightly call you so, and that you permit me to do so, that gives your answer to me at once that you love me with all your heart. I have just found the little request on the envelope ["si(gk5f6K5E—41icge7"] and you see I am obeying at once. I have just returned from Capt. Kenedy where I went since supper with your mother's answer to my telegram and now I have come to my room to have a little chat with you, my own precious darling. First I want to kiss you for being so good & writing me a letter on Sunday. You stated in your letter of Saturday that I must not expect a letter from you but I could not be fooled that way. I went to the post office with all the confidence in the world expecting my Sunday letter. You see, I am right. Never despair. Never look at the dark side of anything until you are compelled to do so. I am making good use of this pencil to remind me of our little trip together. I think of our last moments together. They were sad in some respects because we were parting, but in others they were of the happ[iest] of my life. Never can I forget your dear mother's blessing and pressure of her hand when I had kissed you, my own precious one, in her presence and I shall certainly do my best to prove worthy of the trust she has placed in my keeping and that which you, Darling, have placed in my care—your happiness and very life. All I ask is an opportunity to prove my worthiness. How my heart fills with sweet emotions of happiness at the thought that some day, my little Darling, my Little heart, will also be my precious wife. Then I can prove all my professions. Then I can help my Little Heart to bear the ills and burdens of life so much better even than I now can, for when others are near us I must always look on like an uninterested observer. Never mind, Little Heart. The time will soon pass when we must meet as strangers before others.

Your nice long letter is a good consoler for me when I think of the visit of the other young attorney who did not come quite soon enough to keep my little heart from going pitty-pat for me though far away on the borders of civilization. I wrote your mother last night asking her not to go to Va unless Richard could go with her and unless she felt stronger than she has been feeling since she left and I agree with you that it will be better for her to go [to] Ky? Besides she would perhaps find her old friend so engrossed with her family duties or, in other words, so much married that she would not be as she used to know her & then she would feel disappointed and she would not enjoy her visit there. I think next year she ought to try Saltillo, Mexico. I have known several ladies who suffered from nervous prostra-

tion like your mother and yourself who were so much benefited by their stay there even for a short while. Only one instance I remember particularly, Mrs. Geo. Fulton, Jr. She had lost one of her children and had been so grief stricken by it that they almost despaired of her recovery. She suffered principally from nervous prostration and want of appetite—and there seemed to be something in the purity—purity of the mountain air there that soon restored her appetite and with it came new strength—and she soon recovered entirely. I met her at Ingleside on my recent visit there & she seemed just as healthy and strong as ever.

You ask me if I knew when I would go to Brownsville and I do not know but I am going to Santa Gertrudis Monday morning and stay there for several days as Charley Blucher has some surveying to do that will keep him busy for some three or four days and besides, I cannot leave now until I close a transaction with Mr. Carson.

Charles Blucher was the son of pioneer surveyor Felix Blucher.[70] The estate of Richard King owed Thomas Carson, representing Stillman interests, considerable sums. Carson later was also one of the organizers of the St. Louis, Brownsville & Mexico Railway.[71]

I will surely take a "rest" in the hammock on the good old porch at Santa Gertrudis—and oh how I long for someone there to bring me ginger snaps and some one that I could make perfectly "furious"—the little cowhide will be hanging in the same place and I think I would be only too glad to have a little Tyrant strike me with it. The thought of all these things makes me homesick. How much more will I miss you when I find the place all deserted. I fear, my little Heart, that I will not be able to make my visit home as soon as I expected nor have I heard lately. One reason, I presume because I have been too busy to write them lately and then I could hardly have the heart to tell them that I was not coming as I had expected for I know it will be a sad disappointment to them. I will not tell them this until I know all hope of my visiting them is lost.

Now good night, my own precious Darling. How the days seem to drag until I can clasp my own true noble Alice to my breast. Do not form too many resolutions for the future. We will first take in the situation before we make any rash promises. I may not be able to be with you so very much during the coming winter that you must prepare beforehand toward offering to demonstration [sic] devotions. We will not cross that bridge until we get to it.

Speaking of bridges, that reminds me of the fact that the bridge has been repaired and that we can find the way across the creek now and we can retreat to the good old confidant—the old mesquite tree—if the little nieces & nephews are too curious.

The opposite bank of Santa Gertrudis Creek was a place where Robert and Alice would go to be alone together.

Now good night again my own precious Alice. "Kiss" May God keep you harmless and return you to me soon. Give my love to your mother. I will write her again soon. Goodnight (Kiss) oh what an unsatisfactory kiss, but this is all I can impart now & with it, remember, comes my undivided boundless love for you.

Yours always

Robert

❧

[Sent to] Miss Alice G. King, 3815 Delman Avenue, St. Louis, Mo.

Wednesday morning Santa Gertrudis Sept. 9th, 1885

My Dear Little Heart

Such [a] night I had. Just begun writing to you when Don Reuben came in and remained until nearly 12 P.M. so I took up what I had written & considered I had best wait until next mail before writing to you as your mother's letter of last night would tell you that I was still among the living & loving. *This morning I find the mail bag still there as they have not been in the habit of sending for the mail until evening. So I conceived while I was waiting for breakfast I would drop a note at least to my little Pet as I am going out immediately after breakfast to the Leoncitos League.*

Robert had taken to calling Alice his "little Pet," which is what Richard King called his children, particularly Alice. "Don Reuben" was Reuben Holbein. As agent for Richard King, he had managed several large wagon trains of cotton to Brownsville during the Civil War. After the war he became a regular employee at Santa Gertrudis. He was at King's deathbed in San Antonio and began helping Henrietta and Robert manage the rancho.[72]

Somehow, Darling, I don't care to stay about this house as much as formerly & I prefer being out driving. Can you understand why? Oh, I cannot tell you how much I miss My Little Darling. This is the first time since I learned to love my Little Pet that I have remained here for any length of time when she was absent & I can tell you it does not seem like the same place to me—but I am not going to permit myself [to] feel any more lonesome than I now do by permitting my memory to run away with me this early in the day. Tonight will be plenty of time for that so I will tell you of yesterday.

I went out with Mr. Doughty to the Fitch Pasture and on the way there while crossing the woods I saw a large bunch of turkeys & of course I at once attacked them & had to run about ¼ of [a] mile before I regained sight of them again & then I fired & killed one. This paid me for my morning's trip.

Fitch Pasture was probably named for Captain John Fitch, a ranch foreman and trail boss for King on cattle drives. The area that came to be called Fitch Pasture was where the cattle were gathered before being driven north.[73] Previous letters have alluded to the fact that Robert was an avid hunter. King Ranch offered him plenty of space in which to hunt and plenty of wild game.

We did not get back to the Ranch until after two—got dressed & wheeled the old reclining chair on the front porch, took all the papers out with me and in a few moments read myself to sleep & oh what sweet dreams soon came to me. They brought my Little Darling to me & I felt her loving lips on my forehead when I awoke, almost ready to reach out my arms for you. I don't know what awakened me. Your spirit, I think. Well the bell has just rung & I must say adios (Kiss Kiss Kiss Kiss) with all my heart and soul

Your lover

Robert

[Sent to] Alice G. King, 3815 Delman Avenue, St. Louis, Mo.

Wednesday night

Santa Gertrudis, Sept. 9th, 1885

My Own Precious Alice

I wrote you a short and hurried note this morning—and I expect one such a scrawl a day is about as much as you can stand, but I know you have always been very considerate to me in the past, putting up with so many of my short comings so I will trust to the generosity of your nature this time and afflict you with another scrawl.

Don Reubin has just made his appearance in the Hall and is walking up and down with the majestic strides of a pent up bear, just as he did last night, but he shall not prevent my writing you this time. I shall give him about 30 minutes & then resume this letter.

Robert was writing from Santa Gertrudis, and the details in this letter suggest that he was in charge of operations at King Ranch by this time. He was also apparently still heavily involved in his law practice. He was thus a very busy man. Perhaps Reuben Holbein was concerned about this new manager of the rancho, hence the pacing while Robert was writing his letters.

> *Well here I am again after about an hour. He had a telegram for me from Mr. Carson informing me of the arrival at Corpus by night's train of Don Bernardo Yturria who has come up on business with me. I have wired him to come out here as I am not ready to transact his business just at this time—but you do not care to hear all this long business matter.*

Don Bernardo Yturria was the brother of Francisco Yturria, who began his career clerking for Charles Stillman, a powerful businessman in South Texas and former partner to Kenedy and King until 1865.[74] Yturria became part of the King and Kenedy ranch operations along with Stillman. The Yturria family became very wealthy from its many business enterprises along the border in Brownsville and Matamoros.[75] The Yturrias were also the bankers for Kenedy and King.[76]

> *Well, I went out this morning (here comes Mr. Doughty—he thinks I am lonesome and that he ought to talk to me—but I shall get through with him in a little while—tell him I have some letters to write). Well I shall start again, for I will tell you of the days doings. I started to the Leoncitos on dry creek tank took [Dudley?] & Mr. Doughty along to determine upon best moves and place of repairing or rebuilding the tank there which was washed away by the heavy rains this summer.*

James M. Doughty, the old Texas stockman who had been one of King's foremen and herd bosses on the roads to Kansas, had been put in charge of the ranch during the captain's last illness. Kleberg retained Doughty as a personal assistant and superintendent of range work. Doughty then brought in his son, A. C. "Mack" Doughty, and made him one of the foremen in charge of infrastructure. Robert was probably referring to the elder Doughty in his parenthetical comment and Doughty the younger later on, as that mention pertains to tanks.[77]

> *We had two of the young horses in a [jitney?] and away we went. I took my gun with me again and we had not gone more than about a mile or two from the ranch when a wandering[?] coyote sneaked across our path. I at once began the attack and before the wolf knew it his legs failed to sustain him and he fell. I jumped out and found that I had wounded him but he was not dead so I put the heel of my immense boot upon his head a few times as he soon was dead and his soul in his happy hunting grounds. I scalped him and on we went—in full tilt—until we reached the San Fernando.*

San Fernando is a creek that is part of the old Rincón de Santa Gertrudis grant.[78]

> *"Andres" was driving and though there was considerable water in the creek he drove in and when the horses got about half way across down they sank into the mud. They floundered around and one horse soon got loose from the harness & struggled out to the bank—but the other horse could not get out of the harness. Finally Andres got him loose and out the second horse struggled. All passengers except my dogs Dick & Dock had to get out and wade out through mud & water. Then they hitched the horses to the buried axle of the wagon & pulled it out backward. We soon were on our way again, found a better crossing and got over the San Fernando all right that time, took in the situation at the tank and returned to the Ranch. On my way back I killed a new mess of Plovers and at about 2½ we were back all safe sound and hungry, but we had my turkey*

for dinner. It was fine. I then adjourned to the front gallery wheeled out the big reclining chair and had a glorious nap (the hot weather is breaking, I think, for the summer).

This evening I went out again for a short drive to train my dog—after quail—had a nice drive. My dog did finely. Think he will make a good dog but I had rather taken a drive in the old big carriage with you and your mother. So it is, we never know how much we enjoy a thing until after it is past & we can't enjoy it again. Then we feel that if we had just another chance we would certainly enjoy & appreciate the opportunity so much more, though I certainly have enjoyed the quiet drives at the ranch with you and your mother, the many little walks down to the old creek or to the bridge. By the way, the bridge is rebuilt, a suspension bridge one span across the creek. I looked for your little seat near the bridge but I think it has been moved, but Darling of all the different objects in this old hall there is none that reminds me of you like your little rocking chair. It is sitting near me now. What would I not give if the owner would only come and sit in it even if she remained ever so quiet. (Here comes Don Reuben again. The spirit of restlessness must be possessing him. He has taken up his time of march again with solemn stride.) So I might as well give up the idea of writing more tonight.

Good night, my own precious Pet. What an unsatisfactory good night this is when you are away from this old house so many miles. May He always protect you and bring you and your good mother safely back to me is my prayer tonight and believe me as ever forever yours with all my heart & all my life. Love—

Robert

❧

[Written on Menger Hotel stationery. Envelope not available.]

Menger Hotel
Curlis Davis Manager
San Antonio, Texas Nov. 3rd 1885
My Darling Little Pet:

It is late now and I am a little wearied and feel like resting but I think I will feel a little more like I could sleep quietly after saying good night to you and acknowledging the receipt of the nice lunch you sent me to Collins, and the dear letter you sent with it. I was hungrier for that than for the lunch, though I had failed to get my breakfast before leaving Corpus. I [presumed?] because I had failed to get my little supper of Kisses the two nights before, so I find the packages & took out my letter, and devoured it the first thing, and while it filled me with happiness it also gave me a strong touch of homesickness when you told me of the little delegation of two sitting in the hall the night before and of the little girls with eyes filled with tears and I not there to kiss them away and of the little walk with your mother in the evening. Oh, my little Alice, I don't think that I would ever grow tired of sitting in the old hall or taking little walks to the good old Santa Gertrudis Creek if you were only with me, for it surely gives me great pleasure to share your quiet life in the country with no one near us but your dear mother, whose presence seems to shed a halo over it all, than to jossle [sic] *along the busy streets of crowded cities crowded with people who are nothing to me & I nothing to them, or to travel among the loveliest scenes which must always be lacking the chief attraction when you are not there. And it is more pleasure to me and gives my inward longings more comfort to talk to you, Darling, and hear you talk of all the little every day occurrences around your home—of your love for me—than to hear the wisest statesmen or scholars speak of the great events that are daily occurring in the outer world. All these things at last only seem to be of interest to me so far as they can have any bearing or influence on my little Heart's life and love for me, for that is more to me than all the rest, but you do not care to hear any more of my likes and dislikes, and besides I did not say that I was going to speak of anything this time but the little lunch. I enjoyed it every bit. I made my dinner and supper out of it with a friend on Monday & today I made my dinner off of it and I had some ginger cakes left for a lunch tonight. I truly wish I could open my desk tonight and take a cake out of it. I think it would taste a little better in the old Hall than away out here. I also had that portion of your friend's letter enclosed in yours. I agree with her, Darling, that horseback riding would be more beneficial to you, only I am always afraid that [illegible] might move a little too quickly for you sometime and hurt you, and then I would never forgive myself for permitting you to ride him for I know you will never ride him against my wish but we will find some way for you to take horseback rides to suit us both.*

Robert was concerned about Alice's horseback riding, although she had been on horses all her life.

Now, my Little Heart, I must bid you good night. I will have to be fresh in the morning for work in court. I will write to your mother tomorrow evening. Give her my love. May God watch over you both and keep you harmless is the prayer of your Robert, who loves you more than he can ever tell

RJK

[No envelope available.]

The Myrtle Club
Corpus Christi, Texas

Corpus Christi, Dec 7th 1885

My Precious Little Tyrant

I cannot tell you how much I sympathize with you in your illness & how disappointed I was that I did not get my letter tonight, but your good mother had the kindness to write me a little note telling me how her little "chick" is getting on & while nothing gives me more pleasure than your letters, still, Darling, I would not for one moment wish you to visit while you are too ill to do so without impairing you. Our *good mother will keep me posted and I have authorized her to do my scolding & petting while I cannot give the matter my personal attention, my most pleasant occupation.*

By this point in their relationship, Robert was referring to Alice's mother Henrietta as "*our* good mother," a sign of his growing intimacy with the family.

Now, my Little Heart. I am only sending you this little short note because Richard is with me and I think he now is growing sleepy and as he does not take any interest in whist & card games I am going to take him to my room and here we will have a long talk.

Richard King, Alice's brother, was visiting in Corpus Christi.

Now good night, my own precious Heart. God Bless you and keep you free from harm and may he soon have you restored to good health again. I am going to do some little praying now for you as you did for me while I was in San Antonio, though I fear my prayers will not be heard as well as yours were. Still, what my praying lacks in merit, my subject is better & more deserving. Good night again & [I] send you a thousand kisses, each as a message to tell you that I love you, my little Heart, with all my life. Your Robert

[No envelope available.]

Tuesday Corpus Christi Dec 8th 1885
My Own Precious Alice—

Tonight I was made happy by the receipt of your letter commenced on the 6th and finished on the 7th, and while I can well imagine how ill my own little heart must have been not to have been able to write to me on Sunday, it also shows that she was a little better on the following day. Now, my Little Heart, while there is nothing that gives me greater pleasure when I am away from you than to receive a letter from you, still I would not have you make yourself worse by taxing your strength too much in writing to me, for your good mother will write me and tell me how you are getting on and then when you are well again I shall insist on your making up your short coming in writing.

Now, my Little Heart, I am not going to quarrel with you now about what you say about my giving you presents. I will explain the propriety of that when you are well and will content myself at this time by not saying anything more than to express my unqualified sanction to your using the little writing desk just as often as you possibly can when you are well enough. In writing me such long letters, one thing is certain, I am improving in the selection of my presents. I think the desk was just what you needed as a reward for the many good, and to me, dear letters you have written me, and the little glass is just the thing of all others that I should do without, according to your judgment; but I am going to wait with my explanations.

Robert gave Alice a writing desk that she perhaps protested as being too extravagant a gift. His letters have repeatedly suggested that Alice was not writing to him as often as he would have liked. Apparently, he hoped to solve that problem with the writing desk. Doing without "the glass" was perhaps a reference to his abstaining from alcohol to satisfy her wishes in that regard, or perhaps the desk had a mirror with it and refers to conceit.

> *I only wish I could be near you to pet you, my own precious little Pet, and show you how deeply a truly loving heart can sympathize with you. I feel it more every day, that I am but poorly repaying you for the wealth of love you have shown me and given me by simply returning that love with all my heart, for I should be near you now, my little Heart, to comfort you and nurse you and cheer you. How I wish I could give you that kiss on your throbbing temples.*

Alice had apparently been suffering more migraine headache pain.

> *Never mind. All will come right in the sweet by and by and then I will help you, and Richard has been with me all day. We have been buying one thing and another all day long. The rest of the time we have spent in the Myrtle Club & he seems so much pleased with it that he has made application to become a member. He is stopping with me and while I am writing this he is talking with Dr. McGregor in the next room. He leaves for the Puerta in the morning. I expect to go out to see him Friday for a hunt and take some friends with me for a quail hunt.*

Robert and Alice's brother, Richard, were apparently becoming good friends. The Dr. McGregor visiting with Richard King II was W. W. McGregor, physician and photographer and a member of the Myrtle Club, which no doubt Richard was questioning him about. The club roster included influential early citizens.[79]

> *I wish I could go to see my little heart instead, but I can't well do it* our *mother to nurse and comfort one another [*sic*]. I wish I had nothing else to do and was at perfect liberty to do all for you that I would like.*

By tonight's mail I also received your kind letter of the 3rd and the other one you wrote to me at Cuero. So you see, my little pet, your letters come in good time, just when you are not able to write. I also received one from Capt. K., which I enclose for your mother. It was written by his nurse and signed by himself. I hope he will be here the day after tomorrow night but without giving offense.

The *Corpus Christi Caller* reported around this time that Captain Kenedy was in San Antonio and was unwell.

Now Good Night, little pet. God grant that you may be well again by this time at least, that that miserable old headache has left you long before this reaches you. I am going to enclose just a little note to your good mother. You will not grumble at that because I have on several occasions enclosed notes to you in her letters. Good night again. Take good care of yourself, my own precious little Heart, and get well just as soon as you possibly can & then don't get sick any more. That is my order. *Yours with a heart full of love for you only Robt.*

❧

[Addressed to] Miss Alice G. King, Collins P.O., Nueces Co., Tex.

Corpus Christi Dec 10/85
My Own Precious Alice—

I have so often tried to tell you with what perfect happiness it fills my heart to be able to say those four words and to know that it is me and that you delight in hearing me call you so. This almost sounds like conceit, and it certainly is enough to make any one conceited. Still, my Little heart, I do not hesitate to talk to you as I would to myself. I cannot in fact keep from confiding to you my most innermost thoughts and emotions, and so I must confess that I do feel a little conceited just on this one point. And I cannot understand why one so undeserving as

I should have been so favored as to win your love, my precious heart, for I believe with Schiller—"that to win the one love of a pure and good woman is the greatest achievement of mans life"—but while I feel that I have been successful in this, there is still one greater achievement, and that is for a man after having won such a love to prove himself worthy of it—and that, my little Heart, shall be my highest ambition and I feel that there is nothing so great or good which I could do in this life which would be more than your love for me deserves.

Johann Christoph Friedrich von Schiller (1759–1805) was a German poet, philosopher, historian, and playwright. Schiller wrote essays discussing issues of aesthetics.[80] Robert was quoting from *Literary and Philosophical Essays,* indicating that he read some very heady material in his spare time.

So you must not feel gloomy or discouraged because you do not feel so strong yourself at this time for you are the main spring to all my actions, and my good health and strength are yours and the knowledge that you truly love me makes me wonderfully strong.

I am going to the Puerta in the morning. Mr. Atlee McCampbell is going with me. It seems that no one else is able to get off just at this time. We will hunt until Saturday evening & take the train back to Corpus that evening.

Atlee McCampbell was a member of the Myrtle Club.[81] He lived next door to Mifflin Kenedy on the bluff in Corpus Christi.[82]

I am sorry that I will have to miss my letter for one day—Friday. But you are perhaps right, my little heart. My cold is much improved and I hope that by this time you will have reserved your throne & scepter and Key—Your greatest ornament in the way of dress.

Capt. Kenedy did not come tonight, his doctors having ad-

vised him to remain until Sunday. Now good night, my little Heart. I have several other letters to write tonight & it is growing late for one who has to rise at 6 in the morning. Take good care of yourself and obey all our *good mother's instructions & I am sure you will soon be well again. God bless you. With purest and deepest love for you alone.*

Your Robert

[Addressed to] Mrs. H. M. King, Collins Nueces [torn]
[This letter to Alice would have been enclosed in the envelope addressed to Henrietta King.]

Corpus Christi 12/22/85

My Own Precious Little Heart

I am again waiting for the arrival of the train and the letter which I think it is carrying for me, and I shall wait to get it before I start for the concert, company or no company, and though it may be a short note still I shall not deny myself the pleasure of reading it just to be prompt. My excuse will be, if I am late, which I expect to be, that [I] was compelled to await the arrival of the mail in order to get my mail in which I expected a letter of importance, yes that little letter will be of considerable importance, so much so that I should be disappointed in and not receive it. I will not be in a good humor to enjoy the concert nor will I be as agreeable to my company. So Miss [Heaney? Hennie?] should not complain at my tardiness.

Your little note contained but a few words but it told me what above all things I wanted to read in your hand writing, that you love me—and that you are well and if I get the same news tonight again I will be in a good frame of mind to enjoy myself, to be agreeable to those whom I may chance to meet. I send you enclosed a program of tonight's entertainment.

The train has arrived. I heard the whistle as I began this note. So I must close and go. My friend Dr. McGregor is better today. Poor fellow he has a very uncertain future to look forward to. What a blessing good health is. I thank *God [I] am as well as a fish, am free of my cold at last so that I will be in good [trim?] for Santa Gertrudis Thursday morning—and having arrived there we will have that little walk which you promised down to* our *old mesquite tree.*

The *Corpus Christi Caller* had the following notations about McGregor. On January 24, 1886, it reported that "Dr W. W. McGregor returned from his trip to the country looking much improved. It is stated on good authority that he slaughtered an alligator in one of the Puerta lakes that measured 15 feet. The monster was brought to the Puerta ranch & exhibited." On March 7, 1886, the newspaper stated that "Dr. McGregor is visiting the Puerta ranch. He has greatly improved since leaving the city."

Good night, my own Darling Alice. God bless you and preserve you for him who loves you with all heart & life.
Your Robert

My Little Pet

[Addressed to] Miss Alice G. King Collins Nueces Co. TX
[Written on Law Office stationery from the Marcellus Kleberg firm.]

Law Office of
M. E. Kleberg
Galveston January 6, 1886
My Dear Little Heart,
While it gives me pleasure to write to you at any time, it gives me still greater pleasure to answer a letter from you but as the letter is out of the question, I shall take advantage of the

> *present missive to indulge in the pleasure of telling you what I feel [torn and illegible] what I have been [torn and illegible] to you so is missing and I have you, my own precious heart, with all my life and I miss you so this evening.*
>
> *How [I] wish you were here with me tonight & that you could attend the opera with me and hear Emma Abbott in* Linda *in which she sings [O luce de quest anima?].*

The opera *Linda de Chamounix* contains an aria in the first act, "O luce de quest anima" (O star that guid'st my fervent love).[83] Robert was no doubt referring to this aria when he implied that hearing it in the performance that night would make him think of her.

> *Tonight I have for my company my brother Rudolph, the one who lives in Cuero. He arrived here last night on his way to Brownsville where he is going to stay with Judge Turner to attend Federal Court. It was quite an agreeable surprise to us all to meet here together—the first time that we have all three been together for three years.*

Robert was referring to Judge Ezekiel B. Turner, who came to Texas in 1853, moved to Austin in 1854, and practiced law there until the Civil War.[84]

> *Tomorrow night Mrs. Judge Stayton is going with me to hear* Norma. *She and the Judge arranged last night another pleasure for I had not met her for nearly eighteen months. She I used to call her my other mother. The next night I shall take my sister-in-law to the opera. The last & fourth night will be* Faust. *So you see I will have an opportunity of enjoying the opera to my heart's content.*

The *Galveston Daily News* reported on Friday, January 1, 1886, that the Emma Abbott Opera Company would be appearing at Tremont

Opera House. The notice indicated that the operas to be performed would be *Linda de Chamounix, Bohemian Girl, Norma, The Mikado,* and *Faust.* According to his letter, Robert was planning to see at least four of those: *Linda, Norma,* and *Faust,* plus the unnamed opera he planned to attend with his sister-in-law.[85]

> *No not that either for there's another side reason[?] [illegible] for the second night on compan[?] for me [without argument?] you. I am at work during the day [busy?] preparing an argument for my motion on a hearing of my last case. Well here it is again a delegation of brother attorneys. So I must close for now. The callers are gone but it is time for the opera So good night & when I hear sweet [illegible] my thoughts will turn to you and a little air castle rising up in the mist of the distant (?) future. May God keep you harmless. Give my love to your dear mother and believe me to be as ever and forever your devoted lover*
> *Robert*

❧

The following poem, included with Robert's letter of January 6, 1886, was copied onto mourning stationery.[86] The author of the poem was Annie Shepherd Swan, a Scottish writer, and the poem is from the book *Marion Forsyth: Or Unspotted from the World.*[87] Robert perhaps hoped the verses would be a comfort to Alice, still mourning the loss of her father.

From the Depths

In this sad world of ours—
The dreary wilderness of care & pain,
This mystery, this turmoil of unrest,
This rough & stony pathway to the tomb,
Where many tears & blurring shadows fall—
How sweet, O Lord, to know that we are Thine.
That in thy hand this mighty chaos lies,

That thine the key of this great mystery—
We could not bear it else!

For as the years go by
One sorrow makes a strange, preparèd way
For yet another; one by one our joys
Are wrested from us ere we call them ours;
And sweetest human ties are severed wide.
And sweetest human cares slip from our grasp;
And dear home nests are robbed of all the birds,

And family trees are stripped of flower & leaf;
And many graves lie greenly side by side,
And oceans roll between some we hold dear—
Till with sad folded hands we sit and say,
How can God have it so?
For human hearts will cry out for their loves,
And human eyes seek dumbly for the smiles
Of angel faces gone.

God pity us!
Oh wrap us in the fulness of Thy love!
In infinite compassion lay Thy hand
Upon our hearts and make them very still
And since the cross is Thine, oh help us bear
It very patiently, until that blessed morn
When all the shades of night shall flee away,
When we shall clasp again the loved & lost,
And every severed bond shall join again;
Where in the light that circles round the throne
In all His beauty—All shall see the King!

[Addressed to] Miss Alice G. King, Collins, Nueces.
[Written on Stayton & Kleberg Law Office stationery.]

Law Office R. W. Stayton, Victoria
Stayton & Kleberg R. J. Kleberg, Corpus Christi
Victoria and Corpus Christi
Corpus Christi, Texas Jany. 22nd 1886
My Own Precious Alice—

You must pardon me for using this business paper to write to you for I was compelled to borrow a little of the night to finish my day's task so I am in my office. I have no other letter paper here & I assure you that a little chat with you tonight in this place has a very cheering effect on me. I feel that after the days labor is over I have someone to turn to for a few pleasant moments—someone who has been with me all day but while I was conscious of her cheering presence I could not take the time to say anything to her until now that I am alone in my office with the key turned in the door & now I am going to tell her first about my new room.

I moved my furniture & put down my carpet yesterday & today I have it all arranged & fixed up. All this I did by proxy of course for I had neither the time nor the inclination to attend to that part of the performance except to drop in occasionally and see how things progressed. I went up about 12 today and found every thing in ship shape but my company the Dr. had not been in so I went up to Mrs. Mallorys' where I found him still in bed suffering from a stiff neck. I was only too glad that it was nothing worse & stayed to dinner and now I have just returned from another visit to him as he sent me word that he expected to go out in the morning.

The "Dr." is perhaps Dr. W. W. McGregor, whose health was apparently fragile.

I came just a few moments too late for supper but I remained a few moments and chatted with him, Mrs. [D Hayney?] & Miss [Heaney? Hennie?] until train time and then I had the cheek to think that perhaps I would find a letter from my little pet at the post office & sure enough it was there & such a nice good letter too it was. Just what I had looked for.

I did not write last night as I had a number of letters to write & then I thought, well tomorrow I can't look for another letter so I will wait until then & I will write one if I can't read one, but you see I did not know myself; for tonight I was on hand in time at the post office so that if there should be a little letter for me it would not have to wait one moment.

You have doubtless just about returned from your little trip by now & are now talking to your friend. She is in her room. Will she see an old picture hanging near the door of your room & your mother's? If so, what are you going to say about it? Will you blush & smile at the warm tender thoughts which it will kindle in your heart? Ah how I wish I could be there to speak for myself, not that you will not fully represent me, I fear only too generously. If you speak of me do not say too much for your friend might be disappointed when she sees me.

The old picture hanging near the door of Alice's room and Henrietta's is perhaps the photograph Robert had made by Louis de Planque.

I did not like the looks of the saddle I had. I was afraid it might not be good and strong so I sent out a new one which I think is much better & I am sure safer for I can't tell what horse it will be placed on. I have nothing to say on the subject of horseback rides. I fear I have already said too much. I feel just as I imagine you felt when I made an honest confession to you not long since & as you were so good and forgiving on that occasion I haven't the heart to be otherwise, but do be careful, darling. What a terrible thing it would be if something were to happen to you & all just for the sake of a little ride! I presume I have an antipathy to your riding anything but the very safest horse.

Well, Darling, I must close this now for I have a number of other letters to write, one to our *own* good dear *mother so buenos notches* [sic] *God bless & protect you & watch over the horse you ride & may I soon have the pleasure of being with you, my little Pet—my little hertzchen* [Herzchen, *meaning "little heart"*], *my own* True Alice, *so dearly loved by me.*

Your Robert (Kiss)

[Addressed to] Miss Alice G. King, Santa Gertrudis, Collins, Nueces Co. Texas

Corpus Christi, Texas Juary [sic] *26, 1886*

My Own Precious heart

I have just time enough to say good morning and to tell you that I will see you before the week is out, though I cannot say yet what day I will be out—Friday or Saturday, I think—as court has adjourned until Friday & I have no cases set for that day & the prospects are that I will soon be through with my part of court, as most of my cases have been continued already. As I am on the defense in each case, I do not object. Mr. Stayton is here and I will be engaged with him for the balance of the evening as he is going away again on the morning.

So good night, my own true Heart. God bless you & preserve you. I shall answer your dear letter of last night in the morning when I will have more leisure. This is just to tell you that I am well and that I haven't quite forgotten you, that I love you, my own Darling Alice, more & more each day. Good night (kisses)

Yours with a loving heart

Robert

In large writing across the bottom of this sheet is written: "For Little Tyrant."

[There was no envelope with this letter.]

*Corpus Christi, Texas Jany [*sic*] 27th 1886*
My Own Precious Heart

Tonight as usual I was on hand promptly to get my letter and while your letters always seem short to me still I cannot & do not complain for, Darling, you could never write me so lengthy that I would grow weary with reading it as long as I could find a trace of love in it but you must not deprive yourself of any pleasure just to please me by writing to me, for I do not deserve such sacrifices at your hands. Your pleasures at home are but few at best. No, I will not say that either, for I know there is nothing on earth now that you enjoy so much as being at home with your mother and doing little acts of love for her. I know that there is nothing that gives me such true pleasure as to be with those I love & those that love to have me near them, and the simplest little pleasure that I can enjoy with them gives me more real satisfaction than the grandest entertainment can give me when they are not near me. The truth is I am not all anywhere when I am alone and my best part, that which is at the bottom of all my enjoyment, is a little girl that is very [fervent?] of horseback riding & her little request is so tempting that I cannot say no. I ride *with* you. *That is hardly fair—to tell me that you will go with me if you can ride McVoy [?] but I will not discuss that now.*

The ranch offered few pleasures for a young woman like Alice, but horseback riding was one of them. Despite having been raised riding horses, Alice was still having trouble convincing Robert that she could safely ride a horse; she has been asking his permission to ride, and this letter suggests that he had relented somewhat. The issue presents an interesting tug of war between the two and calls to mind the oft-made statement that Alice lived her life for others—first her father, then her mother, and now Robert.[88]

I am going up to see Capt. Kenedy as soon as I mail this letter & I will try & learn from him when he can go out with me. One thing is sure, if he can't go with me on Saturday that then I shall go without him. I shall try to get him to go with me Friday.

By this time Captain Kenedy had become not only a client of Robert and his law firm but also an adviser and surrogate father to him.

Now good night, my own Precious Heart. God bless you & keep you harmless and may He grant that we may soon meet.

I wonder how long your friend is going to stay! I am growing jealous, for court will soon be over & then—then—I will want [to] be near you all the time. Life is no life at all without you. Good night. Give my love to our mother & tell her that I have sent a kiss in this letter to her for you & that she must let you have it. I know of nothing important to [send?] her except that she must keep well.

Your Robert

❧

[No envelope available. This letter was written on Stayton & Kleberg law firm stationery.] R. W. Stayton, Victoria. R. J. Kleberg, Corpus Christi.

Corpus Christi, Texas Feby [sic] *16th 1886*

My Own Precious Alice

Tonight is my night to write you so I will not wait for the train to come in to see if it brings a message for me from you and tomorrow night I am to get your letter. Still I might as well *confess to you at once that I am going to the post office as soon as the mail arrives, for you might have changed your mind or something might have occurred since my departure which would cause you to write—and I would never forgive myself if I would not go to the post office tonight and then in the morning find a little white winged messenger in my post office box—caged there all night—anxious to get to me to impart a certain sweet little story that I never tire of reading or hearing. One thing I am pretty[?] sure of you have not rode [*sic*] the pony since my departure for today has been quite chilly and damp [drizzling?] rain all day. What a blessing it would be if it would only* rain good *a regular log roller and trash lifter.*

The train was about an hour late last night and on my arrival last night I found that both Capt. Kenedy and Dr. McGregor had shaken the dust of Corpus from their feet. The former took the train yesterday morning for San Antonio and the latter left last Saturday for a short visit to Mr. Geo. Fulton's—a cabin on Fultons Pasture—& this morning the Dr., his cousin & Mr. Geo Fulton arrived. I have just left them all in my room. I told them a little white _____ that I had some important business letters to write.

Dr. McGregor, the physician and photographer in Corpus Christi, was also Robert's roommate. Robert was apparently following a genteel custom in refusing even to mention the word *lie;* it would have been acceptable at that time to substitute the word *story,* as in, "Are you telling a story?" or "Are you storying?"

Speak of the angels & you hear the rustling of their wings. Here is one of them now shaking my office door demanding admittance. I will let them in but I must finish this letter. They will not know but that it is on business.

I am going to tell you first how much pleased I am with my pictures. They are very good, I think. I am going to keep yours for you. I shall see if I can find a frame for it. If so, I will have it framed & send it out to you and if you like you can hang it.

The special judge did not come down yesterday and he may not be here for a day or two. If so, I will not get off from here before the end of the week. I shall try and get through with Mr. O'Docherty so that I can go to the Puerta—next week if you go out there—and I will bring with me either Mr. Atlee McCampbell or Dr. McGregor.

Pat O'Docherty was Oscar Lovenskiold's law partner.[89]

Caruthers has gone to Washington to appear before the Harlon committee to tell all of them what he knows about Aransas Pass, so he cannot be at the Puerta.

The Harlan Committee was a congressional subcommittee established to study deep water ports on the Gulf Coast. Robert's good friend W. P. Caruthers was going to appear before this committee regarding the port at Aransas Pass.[90]

But I must close now for my friends are growing impatient. So good night, my own true heart. Be careful about the pony. If he should hurt you—what then? I shan't say. Take good care of your mother and do not fail to bring her with you. Kiss Kiss. God bless and protect you, my own darling Alice, & do you not fail to write me for time hangs heavy without a word from you. Good night Kiss Kiss

Yours with heart, soul & life Robert

In the spring of 1886 Robert was managing not only the King family's legal affairs, with the help of Jim Wells, but also one of the largest ranches in the United States. It covered an area larger than some eastern states; if the land had been located in the East, it would have been large enough to be a state, with its own capitol, governor, and legislature.[91] In order to handle this workload, Robert gathered around him the men who had served Captain King, and he put his trust in them. James Doughty, who had been in charge of the ranch during the captain's last illness, was now Robert's personal assistant and superintendent of range work. Doughty's son Mack became one of the foremen and worked with cow bosses Ramon Alvarado and Jap Clark, as well as horse bosses Luis Robles and Julian Cantu. Robert thus kept many of the experienced personnel on the payroll, but he still had a major hurdle to overcome. The trusted Kineños, King's cadre of workers, had built the ranch with their sweat and expertise, and their loyalty to the captain and "La Madama" was unquestioned. Now there was a new man in charge, and they watched him carefully before extending their loyalty to him. Robert had to earn their loyalty, and earn it he did. Before long they were calling their new *patrón* "El Abogado" (The Lawyer).[92]

Despite his busy schedule, Robert took time to walk with Alice along the banks of the Santa Gertrudis Creek in the quiet evenings at sunset and talk about their future. The couple now had Henrietta's approval and had only to wait until the end of the obligatory year of mourning for the bride's father. So both Robert and Alice attended to their duties, which included helping Henrietta, and looked forward to a time in the near future when they could finally solemnize their union. Captain King had chosen wisely when he took the young lawyer into his household to not only manage his legal affairs and his land but also to throw a mantle of protection around the women he loved most in the world.

Finally, on June 17, 1886, fourteen months after Captain King's death, at six o'clock in the morning in the parlor of Santa Gertrudis, Alice Gertrudis King became the wife of Robert Justus Kleberg. The newspaper reported the marriage as follows: "KLEBERG-KING—At the residence of the bride's mother, Rancho Santa Gertrudis, Nueces County, Thursday June 17, 1886 at 6 a.m., by Rev. J. R. Howerton of Corpus Christi, Mr. Robert Justus Kleberg to Miss Alice Gertrudis

King. No cards. The marriage was very quiet, only Capt. M. Kenedy and Mr. U. Lott, outside of members of the immediate family, being present. The newly wedded couple left at once for the train at Collins, accompanied by Mrs. King, Capt. Kenedy and Mr. Lott. Mrs. King, Mr. and Mrs. Kleberg will go North for a summer trip. The Caller extends its congratulations and many good wishes to the happy couple."[93]

Robert brought confidence, tenacity, a love of intellectual pursuits, a scientific mind, vigor, a sense of humor, and attention to detail to the marriage.[94] Alice brought a strong mind, strength of character, gentleness of spirit, and complete unselfishness.[95] They also brought each other love and respect that had developed over the previous four years, and together they laid the foundation for the dynasty they were to build together.

Robert understood from the beginning the important role that Henrietta played in both Captain King's and Alice's lives. He expressed it well in his letter to Henrietta on October 12, 1884, when he asked Captain and Mrs. King for Alice's hand in marriage. Robert wrote that "no one knows better than I do how well her parents love her and how the declining days of their life are brightened by her presence and devotion—and I can well understand how hard it must be for them to reconcile themselves to the thought that she should divide that devotion with another. Rest assured therefore that I shall never have the heart to ask her to leave you against your consent or wish."[96] Robert never broke his word, and he and Alice lived on the rancho with Henrietta for the rest of their lives.

Robert, Alice, and Henrietta returned from their stay in Wentzville, Missouri, late in the summer of 1886. While they were away, their good friend Emelie Lovenskiold married Thomas Southgate, and again Captain Kenedy gave the bride away, while Mr. Lott followed behind. Returning home, Alice and Robert had friends to greet and duties to assume, but finally they could settle down to uninterrupted time under the same roof surrounded by their South Texas empire.

My Darling Little Wife

[Addressed to] Mrs. Robert J. Kleberg, Collins, Nueces Co.
[Written on Menger Hotel stationery.]

Menger Hotel
San Antonio, Texas Nov. 16th 1886
My Dear Little Pet

I reached San Antonio this evening at 5:40 and after taking my supper called on Rudolph whom I found at his post in his office. With him were several old mutual acquaintances. Among them Mr. [illegible], collector of customs at Eagle Pass, my old room mate at Cuero of whom I have spoken so often, Mr. [Gressen?] little Lina's father. Do you remember the little girl we met at my parents? He looked well and was only [illegible] I did not mention business matters to him, however, & hence did not learn how he was getting on.

While it was quite pleasant to meet old friends it deprived me of the pleasure of talking about home with Rudolph as I would have done otherwise. He is well and hard at work and seemed a little disappointed when I told him that his little sister did not accompany me.

Rudolph was Robert's oldest brother. Lulu was the little sister who did not come.

Old Judge Turner also stepped into Rudolph's room and took occasion to congratulate me and to tell me that he knew I had a very sweet little wife. I told him I knew it too but was glad to get the judgment of the U.S. Court on the subject.

I saw Mrs. Spohn, Mrs. Starck & one of her daughters at the supper table. It seems "the lion and lamb," etc.

"Mrs. Starck" was probably María Vicenta Vidal Starck (sometimes known as Nene), the daughter of Petra Vela Kenedy and Luis Vidal. The daughter mentioned would have been Lillian, who lived with her grandfather, Captain Kenedy, after Petra died, before her marriage to Frank Rabb. The "lion and lamb" was probably Robert's subtle way of referring to the difficulties in dividing Petra's estate between her children with Luis Vidal and her children with Mifflin Kenedy. Sarah Spohn was the daughter of Mifflin Kenedy, while María Vicenta Starck was the daughter of Luis Vidal.[97]

I did not call on them or Miss Lott but asked Mr. L to remember me to his wife.

"Mr. L" was Uriah Lott. With the help of Mifflin Kenedy and Richard King, he had built the Corpus Christi, San Diego, and Rio Grande Narrow Gauge Railroad from Corpus Christi to Laredo. The project required seven years to complete and was jeered as "Lott's Folly."[98]

Also saw Mr. Driscoll & daughter at supper. Did I not see lots of people in a little while?

Robert Driscoll Jr. was one of the incorporators of the St. Louis, Brownsville & Mexico Railway and president of the Corpus Christi National Bank. A close personal friend and business associate of the King family, he was appointed one of two temporary administrators of Henrietta King's will to disburse and receive funds while the will was being probated. The daughter was probably Clara Driscoll (born in 1881), who later achieved renown as the "savior of the Alamo."[99]

The weather was fine today & I wished you and Mother were with me on this little trip but tonight a cold norther is blowing & I begin to think that you are better off at home. I found the trip quite pleasant not fatiguing at all. I only saw Mr. Lott a few moments in the morning. I am to wake at 5 o'clock to take the train for Austin at 6 in the morning. Horrible to contemplate is it not? But if I have good luck I may get back tomorrow evening from Austin & thus save one day in getting home Friday instead of Saturday.

I bought my new hat tonight according to orders, am feeling well but sleepy as it is late, my watch not keeping correct time as usual.

Now, Little Darling wify, good night. How I wish I could be with you in our little room—singing, laughing and talking before going to sleep—but that can't be, so good night, Pet. God protect and keep you [and] Mother safely [sic] *until my return is the prayer of your loving husband,*

Robert

When Captain King died and Robert inherited responsibility for the rancho's operation, he also gained the services of three hundred excellent horsemen, who soon gave their loyalty to the lawyer with a big moustache. They and all of the members of the extended King Ranch "family" expected him to succeed. To do so, Robert exercised his considerable leadership skills. He was fair, deliberate, and thorough, studying the issues and then reaching a conclusion that he expected everyone to respect by following his orders.[100]

It was a difficult time to have inherited responsibility for the rancho because the Great Drought in the Southwest was in its early stages. Robert took stock of the situation and had to alter tradition by stopping the great trail drives and instead shipping the cattle by rail.[101]

Both Robert and his brother-in-law, Richard King II, moved to sell cattle in the fall of 1886. Richard sold a thousand yearlings to A. P. Rachal of San Antonio.[102] Henrietta and Robert closed a trade a couple of weeks later in December and sold fifteen hundred heifers for March 1887 delivery in Colorado.[103]

However, there were many cattle that could not be sold as easily as the heifers. One of the most difficult problems Robert faced was that King Ranch ranges were full of wild longhorns and mustangs that were worth very little yet consuming valuable grass. It took five weeks to clear the board-fenced breeding pasture of wild cattle that had not been worked or branded for several seasons, but finally the job was done and the cattle were sorted and moved out. The vaqueros then turned their attention to the wild mustangs. They built a large enclosure at Tulosa Lake and herded about three thousand mustangs into it. From there, the men were able to load them onto rail cars and ship them to Mississippi and Tennessee. Robert replaced them with a few gentle, well-bred horses to upgrade the stock.[104] Robert also began to buy cattle from breeding farms in Texas, Kansas, Mississippi, Kentucky, Illinois, and Canada. He wanted only the best, scientifically bred cattle for the ranch.

Robert was once asked how much King Ranch land was worth, and he answered that the land wasn't worth anything until you did something with it.[105] With six hundred thousand acres of land but about a half million dollars in debt, the widowed Henrietta worked with Robert to sell off parts of the ranch to friends like Don Francisco Yturria and lawyer James Wells. Through this method, they raised cash and disposed of land that was less important to them, and then purchased land that was more strategically located.[106]

After their return to Texas late in the summer of their marriage, Alice and Robert were able to do some socializing, and in December they, along with Henrietta, were in Corpus Christi after a brief trip to San Antonio.

Robert had to make other adjustments that did not concern business. When he married Alice, he also acquired the longest ruling mother-in-law since Queen Victoria. Henrietta roomed across the hall from Robert and Alice for forty years, she presided over every meal, and she liberally handed out advice to Robert, Alice, and eventually their children.[107] Robert evidently accepted this arrangement and, after his marriage, always referred to her as "Mother." In 1887, the young couple also found themselves expecting their first child, due in November.

Henrietta King in her rocking chair, May 1914, when she was eighty-one. Above the center mirror on an antique dresser is a large portrait that appears to be Henrietta in her wedding dress. On the dresser top are several framed pictures, one of her husband and others that may have been of her father and one of her daughter Alice. Harry Ransom Humanities Research Center, University of Texas at Austin.

[Addressed to] Mrs. Robert J. Kleberg, Collins, Nueces Co

Corpus Christi
July 27th 1887
My Darling Little Wife:

I have just finished reading your most precious and welcome letter—and to prove that you are not tormenting me in writing to me every day, I will tell you that the Hon. Geo P. Finley is now making a speech on the front gallery of the hotel while I have been reading your letter—and am now answering it. So you see I prefer reading your letters & writing to you to listening to the prohibition eloquence of the distinguished orator. He was afraid to permit Judge Hancock to reply to him tonight for he refused to divide time with him.

George P. Finlay was a lawyer, legislator, and former Confederate soldier. He served as Corpus Christi's city attorney from 1885 to 1889.[108] John Hancock was a federal judge and politician. As a member of the Texas Legislature, he opposed the secession of Texas during the Civil War. After the war, he was a Democratic representative from Texas in the US Congress.[109]

I will try Dr. Spohn once more & see if he will say what is best. So far he has said that unless I could get a comfortable and good place for you here you had better remain at home. I hope to be able, Pet, to see you Saturday at 2 o'clock.

Robert was consulting Dr. Spohn because Alice was pregnant with their first child, Richard Mifflin Kleberg, who was born November 18, 1887, in Corpus Christi. Robert was probably trying to make arrangements for Alice to stay in town. Later, in a letter dated August 8, 1887, Alice mentioned that she was having back pains but that the doctor said there was not a problem. She signed that letter, "Your always devoted, Little Wife."[110]

Dr. Arthur Spohn married Sarah Kenedy and was thus Mifflin Kenedy's son-in-law. A well-respected physician in Corpus Christi, Spohn served as the King family's physician and delivered all of Robert and Alice's children. Christus Spohn Health Systems, Corpus Christi, Texas.

> *I am sorry that poor Nettie is so worried about the question left her to decide but it seems to me that any of these places would be preferable to Santa Fe to her. Still, I presume if her husband cannot decide for her, that no one else can.*

Nettie was the sister of Alice who had married an army officer, E. B. Atwood, and was living in St. Louis. According to Tom Lea, "Henrietta's relationship with her daughter Nettie Atwood had been clouded with reserve since before the death of Captain King; though there were exchanges of family news with Nettie, and occasional visits, the bond between Mrs. King and her eldest daughter and family was never as close as with her other children."[111] Nettie had been disinherited by her father, but Henrietta put her back in the will. Robert was referring to a discussion with Nettie over what she wanted as her part of the inheritance.[112] "Santa Fe" was the informal name of the Norias West Ranch, which Richard King II had inherited upon his father's death. The other portion, Norias East, was to be divided into two equal parts. One half was to go to Henrietta Welton Page, sole heir of Ella King Welton. The other one half was devised to the heirs of Nettie King Atwood.[113]

I am glad your miserable cough has at last relented for it worried me and I knew it was so injurious and distressing to you.

Well, Pet, I am writing under difficulties—as [parties?] are moving around so, listening to the speaker, that I cannot write in peace. So I will bid you good night, be careful and to attend the show too frequently [sic] *but as I have been with my old friend Mc[?] for supper I have a first class ticket for a front seat at the show. [It] is a pass to take my spirit to the Santa Gertrudis on wild horses & if I take the trip I think I will see you & not stay out with the horses.*

The old friend is probably Dr. McGregor.

God bless & keep you, my precious wife—with a heart overflowing with tenderest love to you, my little wifie—Your husband

Robert

love to all

[Addressed to] Mrs. Robert J. Kleberg, Collins, Nueces Co Tex

St. James Hotel
Corpus Christi, Tex., August 17th 1887
My Darling Little Wife,

Your dear little note and enclosed letter from Mr. James Hobbs came to hand and in due time tonight & while your note was short still as you say, under the circumstances, it was just what I would have you do. For I know it is not good for you to keep late hours and it told me that you and all others at home are well & that is the main thing.

Mr. James Hobbs was appointed the postmaster at Collins Station on June 16, 1879. Other Hobbs family members at times also worked in the post office and the Hobbs general store.[114]

I am sorry the military were so unchivalrous as to impose on your mother by quartering themselves in [illegible] house without being asked. I am glad their visits are short, few and far between.

Military personnel were apparently at the ranch in order to obtain horses or cattle for the army in fulfillment of contracts already drawn up.

Dr Spohn called on me today for the gray horse I told him he could use so I sent a note by a man today to Mr. Doughty to send the horse down by him. Tell mother about it. I feel it quite important just at this time to keep my promises with the Dr. & to keep on the good side of him. I will make the matter all right.

Robert wanted Dr. Spohn to have whatever he wanted or needed to take care of Alice, who by this time was six months pregnant. The gray horse would have come from King Ranch, where tales were told of a stranger who one evening at dusk had arrived on a large iron gray horse. After accepting Captain King's hospitality for a night's stay, the stranger left on his horse, guided by a Kineño. But the stranger sent the vaquero back on the iron gray horse—a present, he said, from Jesse James to Captain King. Although there was no proof of the man's identity, the horse proved a grand sire for the ranch's beautiful gray horses, commonly known as the Jesse James horses.[115]

> *Now good night, my own true heart. God bless & keep you safe from harm. I think I shall not be able to be home before Friday. If I do not send word to the contrary have conveyance for me on that day.*
>
> *Now Good night again with love for all and for you, my darling wife, from your devoted husband*
>
> *Robert*

At the end of this correspondence, these Victorian lovers, Robert and Alice, had endured the obstacles to their courtship and the tragedies in Alice's family. They were finally wed and soon expecting a baby. The descendants of Robert and Alice Kleberg believed that their love affair lasted their whole wedded life. "Yours until death" was a phrase both used in their letters. It was a relationship that matched that of Captain Richard King and Henrietta Chamberlain in partnership, love of the land, and the continuing and strengthening of a family dynasty that still exists. The union of Robert and Alice ensured the future of that dynasty.

Epilogue, 1887–2011

ROBERT AND ALICE KLEBERG welcomed their first-born child on November 18, 1887. Dr. Arthur Spohn, Mifflin Kenedy's son-in-law, delivered the baby boy in a rented two-story residence called the Greer House on Carancahua Street in Corpus Christi. Robert had found that "good and comfortable" place where Alice could stay while awaiting the birth.[1] They named their first child Richard Mifflin Kleberg, after his grandfather and his grandfather's best friend, Mifflin Kenedy.[2] Mifflin must have been delighted with this little boy who would bear both their names. On November 27 Robert took the time to write to his brother about his new son. The letter was written from Corpus Christi, where Alice was still recovering.

> *Corpus Christi Nov. 27—1887*
> *Dear Rudolph—*
> *While I know that your time is much occupied with the discharge of the duties of your office I know that no news from me at this time is good news; that we are all well but your congratulations were the first to reach us and your letter of congratulations gave us so much pleasure. Alice and our little boy are doing as well as they possibly [can?] both growing stronger each day. The little boy seems blessed with a splendid physique, good looks, his head is large and well-shaped-and adorned by a [tuft?] of dark hair, but his eyes are now gray or blue, it is difficult to see which. His proud mother and mother* [sic] *think*

he favors me very much. I wish you could see Alice looking at her little treasure. She is the personification of a happy mother. Today is the ninth day and so far we have kept Alice perfectly quiet and will try to continue to do so for some days more until she can leave her rooms. Both she and mother join me in love to you, Tillie and the children—Let us hear from you

Affectionately your bro. Robt.[3]

The Children of Robert and Alice

ROBERT AND ALICE went on to have four more children: Henrietta Rosa Kleberg (Larkin-Armstrong), born July 17, 1889; Alice Gertrudis Kleberg (East), born January 9, 1893; Robert J. Kleberg Jr., born March 29, 1896; and Sarah Spohn Kleberg (Johnson, Shelton), born April 12, 1898.[4] The family lived in the enlarged ranch home, and often their cousins from the Agua Dulce Ranch would come for a visit along with their parents, Richard and Lizzie King. Minerva King Patch, Richard and Lizzie's daughter, described the visits. Santa Gertrudis was twenty-five miles from Agua Dulce Ranch, and the family traveled by stagecoach accompanied by a man on horseback who took down fences for the stagecoach to pass and then replaced them. It was a long trip through the sea of grass, mesquite, prickly pear, and occasional clumps of live oak trees. After reaching the Santa Gertrudis, the King and Kleberg cousins would ride horses. The girls could ride side-saddle, but they preferred to ride astride with divided skirts. Each day of the visit usually followed a routine. Everyone was awakened early and served coffee. Then the family gathered for breakfast, a large meal with oatmeal, hotcakes, or biscuits. Then the cousins would mount their horses and ride until noon, when they ate dinner—the largest meal of the day. If anyone missed dinner, there was still always food available; it seemed that the ranch cooks never slept. Dinner was followed by a long nap in rooms shaded by shutters and slats. After the nap there was coffee again, and the grownups would go for a drive in the carriage. At dusk the family gathered for supper, and the evening was spent telling stories and talking about the events of the day. A hunting expedition was an all-day event, with everyone leaving before sunrise and heading out in the buckboard to the designated area. Sometimes the hunters would climb a tree to get a good shot, and ranch workers might rattle a set of deer horns to attract game. The hunting party took food with them and would stay out till dark. They also enjoyed the local version of an English fox hunt—a South Texas coyote hunt—as full of excitement as the traditional ride to hounds.[5]

The five Kleberg children lived at the ranch until they were sent away to school, but in their years on the ranch they developed a love for the land that was theirs, as far as the eye could see. Alice worked hard as a mother, daughter, and wife. She assumed many of Henrietta's duties, which included handling certain business matters and providing hospitality to the many people who came through the gates. Her mother remained in mourning the rest of her life, always dressing in black. She even covered her diamond drop earrings with black enamel and toured the ranch in a mourning-black Rockaway stagecoach. Such was the tone she set. The "Widow King" never allowed alcohol or dancing in her home. Hot as it was, she demanded that the men dress for dinner in tie and jacket, while the women wore corsets, chemises, and heavy gowns. After dinner they would stage family entertainments or sing around the piano, always closing with Grandma King's favorite, "Rock of Ages," while she sat stiffly in her horsehair chair, clutching the family Bible.[6] Henrietta not only wore mostly black clothing but also kept portraits of Captain King prominently featured around the house, wore a brooch with his picture, and kept an image of his face on the Santa Gertrudis letterhead.[7]

Alice and Robert made their home a warm and nurturing place for the children. There was also plenty of nourishment: Robert liked to eat and enjoyed good food. According to Helen Kleberg Groves, "Grandfather Kleberg was a great family man and generally sat down to three huge meals a day. For lunch the kitchen usually served soup, chicken or fish along with two or three vegetables, followed by dessert.

Rosalie von Roeder Kleberg (in cap) and her sons Judge Rudolph Kleberg, Judge Marcellus Kleberg (on his mother's right), with Robert Justus Kleberg and his wife, Alice King Kleberg, standing together behind his mother. The young man is Rudolph Kleberg II. Dolph Briscoe Center for American History, University of Texas at Austin, Texas.

At night there was often dark meat such as venison, beef, lamb or possibly duck and occasionally quail and dove."[8]

Robert had a lively spirit and loved to tell stories and sing. He occasionally would enjoy German beer but was very aware that Henrietta allowed no strong drink in her presence or on her premises. When his own family visited, which they often did, his mother Rosalie would sit at the piano in the music room with her sons Marcellus, Rudolph, and Robert about her as she played and joined her voice with theirs. They often sang old songs in the German tongue of her youth.[9]

It was said that Alice had a warm-hearted gentility about her and carried herself with a generous and sweet-natured grace. She was remembered as an unselfish woman who assumed the duties of motherhood with a deep happiness.[10] According to Helen Kleberg Groves,

> My grandmother, Mana, was physically petite and as I recall always dressed in black or gray. She was constantly mourning the death of a family member. . . . She was a natural-born worrier, and every night before lights-out she went around making sure that the women, children, married couples and their families staying upstairs in the big house were in bed and comfortable. She did not check downstairs because that was reserved for single men and men traveling alone. On one occasion Daddy [Robert Kleberg Jr.] and the men were working cattle at the Laureles Division and camped for the night when a strong norther hit around 2:00 a.m. My father awoke to the sounds of a caravan arriving in camp and Mana had sent out blankets and bed for his comfort. He was outraged and sent them back. He said since the other men did not have these luxuries he didn't need them either.[11]

Although the children could have been considered princes and princesses in their own right, they were not allowed to grow up like that. From the time they were old enough to sit on a horse, they were in the saddle. Alice wrote that when her oldest child, Richard Mifflin, was nine years old, he rode twenty-six miles in a day. At age four, Robert took his first spill from a saddle while urging his pony to gallop. Period photographs show all the children with bird dogs, greyhounds, jersey cows, big bulls, pet lambs, and all kinds of wildlife. They hunted, learned camp crafts, and knew all about the ranch livestock. Although the children all had tasks to perform, they had playtime as well. Their playmates were the young Kineños, and Spanish was the language of the ranch.[12]

In 1893, Richard Mifflin Kleberg was ready to enter first grade, so

Henrietta King built this twenty-room mansion next door to the Kenedy home in Corpus Christi so that the family could live in town while the Kleberg children attended school there. Corpus Christi Public Libraries, Corpus Christi, Texas.

Henrietta built a house in town next door to the Kenedys so that the family could live there while her grandchildren were going to school. Henrietta, Robert, and especially Alice planned the house, which was located at 517 Upper North Broadway. It was a twenty-room mansion with turrets, gingerbread trim, and wooden steps leading down to the bluff. The interior was ornate and extravagantly furnished.[13] While Alice, Henrietta, and the children were in Corpus Christi during each week school was in session, Robert stayed at the rancho and sent lonely letters to his wife and family. Henrietta busied herself with Presbyterian church events and charity work.

Henrietta continued to set the tone for the household, so life was somewhat austere for the family. There were no parties at Mrs. King's home except for those related to charitable enterprises. Sometimes Robert and Alice would go out in society but not very often. Henrietta allowed one subscription to the Corpus Christi weekly newspaper. When each issue arrived, the widow would snatch it, read the gossip, and then sit on the newspaper. Then she would play "guess and tell" until the gossip was exhausted.[14] When the children of Richard King II came to Corpus Christi for weekend visits, particularly during the summer, they would come in from La Puerta on the Tex-Mex Railroad, be met at the station, and then be taken by carriage to their grandmother's Corpus Christi home. The house was near the Presbyterian church where they attended Sunday school, and for the remainder of each Sunday they were expected to remain quiet and rather inactive. Their Uncle Bob (Robert Kleberg Sr.) made their visits a time of fun and treasured memories. He would wake them up early and take them to North Beach to swim in the saltwater surf and play in the warm, wet sand. Sometimes he would take them to visit a nearby farm and pick sweet figs. The highlight of the summer was a trip to Colorado Springs, where the entire family would stay at the Antlers Hotel. Grandmother Henrietta always traveled in a private car.[15]

By the turn of the century Robert and Alice's children were thirteen, eleven, seven, four, and two years old. They all grew to adulthood spending their time both at the rancho and in Corpus Christi. As the nineteenth century came to an end, the Robert Kleberg family was firmly established as one of Texas' most prominent families, and the new century presented the opportunity for them to step onto the national and world stage.

Dynasty

THE TWENTIETH CENTURY brought fame, prosperity, and a new, dynamic generation of Klebergs. In the ten years between Captain King's death in 1885 and 1895, Robert Kleberg worked hard to consolidate the ranch properties, adding valuable pieces of land with the expert assistance of Jim Wells, who joined the law firm of Kleberg and Stayton. Together they handled most of the ranch's business transactions.[16] During that period, not only had the ranch's debts been paid but it had also survived a severe drought, falling cattle prices, and the panic of 1893. In recognition of Robert Kleberg's leadership, on January 21, 1895, Henrietta gave him full and complete power of attorney for all her legal and financial matters. It was a testimony to his hard work, and it secured his place in the ranch's future.[17]

In addition to the debts, the drought, and the bad economic conditions in the country, Robert had struggled with numerous other problems. The native grasses that covered the range when Captain King had bought the land had greatly diminished and been replaced by thickets of mesquite, huisache, and brushy trees, drastically reducing the productivity of the land. The mesquite spread across the landscape when horses ate the mesquite bean pods, which then passed through the animals' digestive systems as they ranged across the land. Even a lack of grassfires allowed the spread of the tangled undergrowth. Robert took up the challenge of clearing the brush by first sending out groups of laborers to chop and clear the brush. Eventually the ranch tried a managed burn program and then went to clearing the land with a specially adapted plow and tractor.[18]

The biggest problem facing the ranch was the lack of water. Robert Kleberg began to study the subject of deep artesian water wells and was determined to try to establish them on the rancho. In October 1898 he read about a deep well drilling machine in Nebraska, and he teamed up with T. L. Herring to bring one to Texas. They started drilling in the spring of 1899, and on June 6, at the depth of 532 feet, the drill reached pure, drinkable water. Word was sent to Robert at ranch headquarters, and he raced to the well with tears flowing down his cheeks. He knew that a new era of ranching had been brought to the Wild Horse Desert.[19] He soon installed windmills and tanks. Robert knew water was the key to developing the entire Rio Grande Valley. Now, with access to water, he could entice the railroads to come, and towns would follow.[20]

With the water problem finally solved, Henrietta King and Robert Kleberg moved quickly to secure both the railroad and the town they had dreamed of. Robert first went to his friend Benjamin Franklin Yoakum.[21] Yoakum in turn went to the undaunted Uriah Lott, who once again was able to crisscross prairie land with miles of railroad tracks. The St. Louis, Brownsville and Mexico Railway was incorporated, with its charter issued on January 12, 1903. The incorporators were Robert J. Kleberg Sr., A. E. Spohn, Robert Driscoll Sr., Uriah Lott,

Carts loaded with pipe at Chaparral and Peoples streets in Corpus Christi. In his first decade of managing King Ranch, Robert Kleberg's biggest accomplishment was the drilling of artesian wells that secured the future of the ranch. These pipes were destined for the new water wells at the ranch. Corpus Christi Public Libraries, Corpus Christi, Texas.

Richard King II, John G. Kenedy, James B. Wells, Francisco Yturria, Thomas Carson, Robert Driscoll Jr., E. H. Caldwell, George F. Evans, Caesar Kleberg, John B. Armstrong, and John J. Welder. The officers were Uriah Lott, president; Robert J. Kleberg Sr., vice-president and treasurer; and John G. Kenedy, secretary.[22] The railroad required both cash and land, and Henrietta King, who owned most of the land the railroad would traverse, donated one-half interest in more than seventy-five thousand acres and the right of way across her property.[23]

The owners of these vast tracts recognized the immense value of having the rails cross their property. On July 4, 1904, Henrietta King rode down to the tracks, where flags waved, cannons sounded, and brass bands played to greet the first train to come into her newly created town of Kingsville. Mrs. King stood in a wagon and said, with eyes moist, "Thank goodness it is here." She had lived on the land for fifty years, and finally the dream of developing the Wild Horse Desert was a reality. The first railroad pass was issued to "Mrs. H. M. King" and the second to "Mrs. R. J. Kleberg & children." No longer was it necessary to travel twenty miles to the nearest railroad.[24]

The town of Kingsville was located at a spot Robert and Henrietta had selected: on a hill three miles from the rancho, where she and Captain King had picnicked as a young couple. Mrs. King gave 41,820.6 acres along the railway route and 34,854.8 acres around the townsite to the Kleberg Town & Improvement Company. Most lots were sold for fifty dollars each, and choice corner lots were five hundred dollars. She also donated forty thousand dollars for a schoolhouse and 660 acres for a college for Tejano children. She saw to it that all buying contracts permanently barred the sale of any alcoholic beverages in town, so Kingsville had no saloons or gambling houses and therefore needed no police force or jail. The town grew quickly, and by 1908 it had two thousand residents and a grand hotel called King's Inn.[25]

Many changes came to the rancho. Telephone lines provided a new era of communications with the outside world and throughout the rancho. Kerosene lamplight had been replaced by electric lightbulbs, and water was pumped to the house and available from both hot and cold taps. Large parcels of land like the Laureles Division were added to the ranch.[26] In the spring of 1902, an Afrikaaner clergyman visiting Texas in the wake of the Boer War in South Africa described his visit to the rancho:

> The tour of the farm was undertaken in a vehicle drawn by Texan horses and driven by a Mexican coachman. The ladies chose to remain in the train as a distance of twenty miles had to be traversed over a bumpy road. The King's Ranch is a million acres, the largest ranch in the United States and the property of one person. After 2½ hours of bumping and rolling we arrived at the farm. The reckless coachman had given free rein over stumps and bumps. Those of us who were used to this sort of driving were amused to see how uncomfortable this made the Dutch journalist. On arrival we saw a borehole

> of 1100 ft. where the water comes from a 4 inch pipe and irrigates the land.
>
> The dwelling house was surrounded by workmen's houses for the Mexicans and white foreman. There is a school taught by a Mexican woman in both English and Spanish. We went to dinner and there were fifteen different courses on the table, all from produce grown and made on the farm. There were six cannon around the castle. The manager[,] Mr. Kleberg, planted carrots, cabbages, and other vegetable and has 75,000 horned cattle and 7000 horses and each year has 1,000 foals and 25,000 calves born.[27]

Sadly, the "castle" met catastrophe a decade later. At four o'clock on the morning of January 4, 1912, a fire, probably started by a disgruntled former employee, burned the grand house to the ground. A pet bulldog awakened two of the Klebergs by pulling at their bedcovers. Two guests, Mr. and Mrs. Jeff Miller, also smelled the smoke and rushed to wake the household, and they all scrambled to safety. One of the Klebergs recalled Henrietta King, still dressed in black, emerging from the burning house with a black bag in her hand. She watched her home, associated with so many memories, burn to the ground. Then, as she walked away, she turned and blew it a kiss. Robert immediately began to think about replacing it. Henrietta told him that she wanted him to "build a house that anybody could walk in in boots." Then she left the rest up to him. He wanted it to be a monument to Henrietta's hospitality. He had recently visited a grand hacienda in Mexico, and for the new house he combined its design with elements of Moorish, California Mission, and Long Island architecture and, of course, the Wild Horse Desert. The new house was of stuccoed concrete so that it would be fireproof. It was a massive baronial ranch house consisting of twenty-five rooms, each with a fireplace and most with private baths. It had Tiffany windows, a marble stairway, and floors of mesquite and ebony wood. The dining room could seat fifty persons, who would be getting the chance to experience the famous King Ranch hospitality. The house was completed in 1915 and stands today as a monument to the legacy of Captain Richard King, who came to the Wild Horse Desert in 1853 and stayed to make it the most famous ranch in the world.[28]

With the water wells drilled and the new house completed, Robert was able to experiment with farming. He planted vegetables such as cabbage and onions, grain for feed, and fruit trees, including date, olive, and citrus groves. He was so successful in these efforts that many consider him the father of the Rio Grande citrus industry.[29]

Robert's agricultural contributions in South Texas did not end with citrus. His water wells and railroad project allowed cotton and dairy farming to begin, and he developed a range grass that could withstand heat and drought. He improved the cattle herds by bringing in blooded stock from Missouri and Kentucky, which led to the development of the Santa Gertrudis breed. He also developed towns along the railroad, supported a deep water port, and, in perhaps his greatest contribution to the cattle industry, developed the "dip" to rid cattle of the ticks that caused Texas fever.[30]

Robert was a man of boundless energy and enthusiasm. He was also both exacting and a visionary, and his ability to work closely with Henrietta allowed them to establish a formidable dynasty. His scientific mind led him to seek ways of making the vast land productive and populated.[31] Above all, he was a family man and completely devoted to Alice, his children, and Henrietta.

For the rest of Henrietta's life after Captain King's death, the ranch was known as the "Widow's Ranch." She outlived him by forty years, and until 1918 she was the sole owner of the ranch. Robert never owned any part of it; his mother-in-law and eventually his wife held the exclusive title.[32] (Henrietta also bore the unofficial title "Uncrowned Queen of the West.") She was above all a God-loving woman who cherished her family, and, at the age of eighty-six, she gifted the homestead of the main headquarters of the Santa Gertrudis, including the Main House Hacienda and the surrounding thirty thousand acres, to her daughter Alice because she had "lovingly and faithfully devot[ed] practically her whole life to my care, consolation and aid."[33]

The architect's rendering of the new King Ranch house, which was to cost about three hundred thousand dollars. Dolph Briscoe Center for American History, University of Texas at Austin.

The massive new King Ranch house was completed in 1915, three years after fire destroyed the original house. Corpus Christi Public Libraries, Corpus Christi, Texas.

Robert Justus Kleberg Sr. in his King Ranch office, May 1914. The photograph in the oval frame on the desk is believed to be of Robert's father. The image is replete with items that were appropriate for a large ranch office in 1914. The book he is reading is titled Meridale Jerseys. The middle book of the three at left is Luther Burbank Methods and Discoveries, Their Practical Application (1913). The large desk blotter was provided by the agent for Aetna Insurance of Kingsville, the town that was once a part of King Ranch. Harry Ransom Humanities Research Center, University of Texas at Austin.

Henrietta died at the age of ninety-two on March 31, 1925. After the captain's death, she had gone about doing good works, donating land and buildings for a town, schools, hospitals, a railroad, and a cemetery.[34] As her body lay in state at the great hacienda on the hill, the news of her death spread across the prairies and to cities near and far. Her family and friends began to gather for her funeral, but the most heart-rending tribute came from the Kineños and their fami-

Shortly before her death in 1925 at the age of ninety-two, Henrietta King was thought to be the wealthiest woman in Texas. Dolph Briscoe Center for American History, University of Texas at Austin.

lies. They came by horseback, wagon, and car. Some of the men rode for two days and nights to get there from her far-flung pastures. The foremen of the cow camps gathered as a group to express their sorrow and, in the ancient style, to pledge their faithfulness to La Madama's daughter, Alice. The funeral was held at the rancho with the Presbyterian minister, Reverend S. E. Chandler, presiding. At the conclusion of the service a cortege more than a mile long moved toward the cemetery, named Chamberlain Park in honor of her father. Accompanying the procession were nearly two hundred vaqueros in their range clothes, riding some of the finest horses in the world. They were seeing La Patrona to her resting place. As the final prayers were said there was a noise at the edge of the crowd, and the vaqueros quietly mounted their steeds. In a gesture from the heart, they silently urged their horses into a dash around her grave, their hats by their sides, in a final salute to the woman who was their friend and champion.[35]

At the time of Captain King's death, Henrietta gained title to six hundred thousand acres; when Henrietta was laid to rest, the Santa Gertrudis comprised almost one million acres.[36] During those years, Robert had earned a place among the great cattle barons of the Southwest. For forty years he lived and worked with Henrietta, and after she died he lived only another seven years, the last three years in a wheelchair due to a crippling stroke.[37] He still had control of his mental faculties, however, and sat in on many of the discussions about the ranch's business; he used a rubber stamp for his signature when he could not sign his name. Alice stayed close by his side and every evening would take him riding to see the land and the world-class Jersey herd he had accumulated.[38]

Robert died on October 10, 1932, in his upstairs bedroom at Santa Gertrudis, surrounded by his loving family. He too lay in state at the "Big House," and one of his Kineños, Cadido Garza, with tears running down his face, expressed the sentiment of many when he said, "Adios, amigo mio." At the cemetery Robert's body was placed in the family plot, and again the vaqueros who had come from throughout the mighty ranch rode in silent tribute by his grave.[39] Robert had lived by the strong belief that "those who possess power, property, or influence must hold it in trust for the use of their fellow man."[40]

Alice died on July 31, 1944, and according to the *Corpus Christi Caller,* "Mrs. Kleberg was described by friends who knew her best as a woman of strong mind and character, but with gentleness of spirit and complete unselfishness. The hospitality of the King Ranch, under her direction[,] was traditional and no one in need was ever turned away empty-handed. 'The coffee pot was always on.'"[41]

Robert and Alice's children picked up the reins and provided leadership on the ranch, in South Texas, and even in Congress—all to ensure that the dynasty their father and mother and grandfather and grandmother had started would continue through the generations to come.

The Empire Continues

ROBERT'S SONS were worthy successors and had been trained well for their positions. When Robert developed palsy in 1916, his oldest son, Richard Mifflin (Dick) Kleberg, was recovering from a near fatal attack of appendicitis, so he decided to bring his youngest son, Robert Jr. (Bob), home from college to manage the ranch.[42] Bob was tutored under his mentors Sam Ragland and Caesar Kleberg.[43] His brother Dick recovered from his illness and went on to serve in Congress for seven terms, from 1931 to 1944.[44] It was he who helped to get official recognition of the Santa Gertrudis cattle breed.

Bob saw to the division of the ranch that had been held in trust under Henrietta's will until 1926. It was a bitter and controversial division, but Bob went on to continue his father's legacy. Under his leadership King Ranch established a number of firsts: first to bring to full development a breed of cattle, the Santa Gertrudis; first to experiment in phosphorus feeding; first to abandon the use of barbed wire and substitute smooth wire fastened to fence posts without staples; first to use the humane and efficient electric cattle prod; first to develop and use the tree-dozer and knife-rooter methods of clearing mesquite; and first to experiment with the propagation of wild game. He went on to develop one of the nation's greatest game preserves and continued to develop range grass.[45]

One of the major factors underlying the ranch's continued success was the oil lease signed with Humble Oil (later ExxonMobil) and later a gas lease that would eventually net the ranch millions of dollars. With this wealth, Bob expanded King Ranch to become a global agribusiness conglomerate operating in nine countries and consisting of fifteen million acres. He walked grasslands around the world and saw his prize Santa Gertrudis cattle grazing in knee-high grass.[46]

Another talent Bob possessed was his eye for horses. Bob bred and raced one of the few Triple Crown winners: Assault won the Triple Crown in 1946, with his jockey wearing the King Ranch Running W on his brown and white silks.[47]

After Bob's death in 1974, family members managed the ranch corporation until outside management was brought in. By 2010, King Ranch had 825,000 acres in South Texas. Its worldwide properties have been sold, and the ranch has sought to diversify its interests. The family company now has 36,000 acres in Florida and is the leading citrus grower in America. It is also one of the nation's ten biggest sugarcane producers and has huge cotton, sod, and milo farms. To quote Helen Kleberg Groves, Captain King's great-granddaughter, "If Captain King sat down with us today, he'd say, 'Well, how are things going?' And we'd say, 'They are going fine. We don't have that many cattle or horses anymore. It is hard to make any money at ranching. We've got hunting leases and citrus groves and sod and cane farms.' He would think we had lost our minds."[48]

Be that as it may, the King Ranch dynasty that began under Captain King in 1853 and thrived under the management of Robert Kleberg and his descendants is still a viable institution. The heirs to the King legacy have continued to act on Robert's belief that "those who possess power, property, or influence must hold it in trust for the use of their fellow man."[49]

Notes

Prologue, 1853–1883

1. Robert W. Stayton, letter to Hon. John A. Mobley, Welder Leshin LLP, Corpus Christi, Tex., December 16, 1957, shared with authors on January 20, 2010.

2. DeWitt County Historical Commission, *The History of DeWitt County* (Dallas: Curtis Media, 1991), 535.

3. Tom Lea, *The King Ranch* (Boston: Little, Brown, 1957), 477.

4. Dick Frost, *The King Ranch Papers: An Unauthorized and Irreverent History of the World's Largest Landholders; The Kleberg Family* (Chicago: Aquarius Rising Press, 1985), 702.

5. Box 2J52, Robert Kleberg Family Papers, Dolph Briscoe Center for American History, University of Texas at Austin (hereafter, Kleberg Papers).

6. Sons of Dewitt Colony Texas, "Robert Justus Kleberg," http://www.tamu.edu/ccbn/dewitt/dewitt.htm (accessed June 28, 2010).

7. Ibid.

8. "Kleberg, Rudolph," *Handbook of Texas Online* http://www.tshaonline.org/handbook/online/articles/KK/fk17.html (accessed March 20, 2010).

9. "Kleberg, Marcellus E.," *Handbook of Texas Online,* http://www.tshaonline.org/handbook/online/articles/KK/fk12.html (accessed March 15, 2010).

10. DeWitt County Historical Commission, *History of DeWitt County,* 88.

11. John T. "Jack" Becker, "J. P. Morris and the Rafter-3 Ranch" (MA thesis, Texas Tech University, 2001), 19–20.

12. Robert J. Kleberg, letter to his parents, July 24, 1881, Special Collections & Archives, Mary and Jeff Bell Library, Texas A&M University–Corpus Christi.

13. "The World's Biggest Ranch," *Fortune,* December 1933, 48–61, 89–90.

14. Don Graham, *Kings of Texas: The 150-Year Saga of an American Ranching Empire* (Hoboken, N.J.: John Wiley & Sons, 2003), 195.

15. John Salmon Ford, *Rip Ford's Texas,* ed. Stephen Oates (Austin: University of Texas Press, 1963), 120.

16. Henry Savage, *For Life and Love* (New York: Rand McNally, 1893), 234.

17. Ibid., 227.

18. Lea, *King Ranch,* 2–5.

19. Jane Clements Monday and Frances Brannen Vick, *Petra's Legacy: The South Texas Ranching Empire of Petra Vela and Mifflin Kenedy* (College Station: Texas A&M University Press, 2007), 34.

20. Lea, *King Ranch,* 418.

21. "World's Biggest Ranch," *Fortune,* December 1933, 11–14.

22. Joseph Martin Dawson, "The Greatest Ranch in the World," *Texas Monthly,* 3, no. 6 (April 1929): 463–70.

23. Savage, *For Life and Love,* 231.

24. Ford, *Rip Ford's Texas,* 104.

25. Savage, *For Life and Love,* 235.

26. Scrapbook of Mrs. Sam Rankin, January 1936, Centennial Clippings, La Retama Central Library, Corpus Christi, Tex.

27. Graham, *Kings of Texas,* 46.

28. Ibid.

29. Lea, *King Ranch,* 67.

30. Caleb Coker, ed., *News from Brownsville: Helen Chapman's Letters from the Texas Military Frontier, 1848-1852* (Austin: Texas State Historical Association, 1992), 6–7.

31. Monday and Vick, *Petra's Legacy,* 36.

32. J. Lee Stambaugh and Lillian J. Stambaugh, *The Lower Rio Grande Valley of Texas* (San Antonio: Naylor, 1954), 145.

33. E'Lane Carlisle Murray, "Recollections of Minerva King Patch," given to Bruce Cheeseman, March 1993, copy given to Jane Clements Monday, 3–4.

34. Ford, *Rip Ford's Texas,* 101.

35. Monday and Vick, *Petra's Legacy,* 63.

36. Helen Kleberg Groves, *Bob and Helen Kleberg of King Ranch* (Albany, Tex.: Bright Sky Press, 2004), 8.

37. Ford, *Rip Ford's Texas,* 101.

38. Savage, *For Life and Love,* 236.

39. "J. A. van Blerk 'Met President Reitz deur Texas,'" trans. Natalie Alice

van Blerk, ed. Martin Staples Shockley and A. Ray Stephens, *Southwestern Historical Quarterly* 74, no. 1 (July 1970): 92, available at http://texashistory.unt.edu/ark:/67531/metapth101200/m1/93/?q=J.%20A.%20van%20Blerk (accessed August 2, 2010).

40. Groves, *Bob and Helen Kleberg of King Ranch,* 186.

41. Savage, *For Life and Love,* 239.

42. Ibid., 238.

43. Ibid., 22.

44. Lea, *King Ranch,* 141, 174, 195, 219.

45. Savage, *For Life and Love,* 233.

46. Ford, *Rip Ford's Texas,* 104.

47. Ibid., 119; Lea, *King Ranch,* 325.

48. Lea, *King Ranch,* 324.

49. Ibid., 291.

50. Joseph A. Dacus and James William Buel, *A Tour of St. Louis: or, The Inside Life of a Great City* (St. Louis: Western Publishing, 1878), 95, digitized by Google Books, http://books.google.com (accessed January 2, 2011).

51. Ford, *Rip Ford's Texas,* 123.

52. Ibid., 125.

53. Lea, *King Ranch,* 351.

54. Ibid., 360.

55. Ibid., 508–509.

56. Ibid., 360.

57. Savage, *For Life and Love,* 22.

58. "Stayton, John William," *Handbook of Texas Online,* http://www.tshaonline.org/handbook/online/articles/SS/fst23.html (accessed June 22, 2010); Robert W. Stayton, letter to Hon. John A. Mobley, Welder Leshin LLP, Corpus Christi, Tex., December 16, 1957, shared with authors on January 20, 2010.

59. Bruce Cheeseman, *Perfectly Exhausted with Pleasure* (Austin: Book Club of Texas, 1992), 20.

60. Ibid., 21.

61. Ibid., 27.

62. Ibid., 28.

63. Ibid., 35.

64. Ibid., 33–34.

65. "Stayton, John William," *Handbook of Texas Online,* http://www.tshaonline.org/handbook/online/articles/SS/fst23.html (accessed June 24, 2010).

66. Monday and Vick, *Petra's Legacy,* 273.

67. Sister Mary Xavier, "Social Life and Activities and Cultural Societies," September 1965, 4, La Retama Local History Center, Corpus Christi Public Library.

68. Quoted in Lea, *King Ranch,* 338.

69. Ibid., 339.

70. Monday and Vick, *Petra's Legacy,* 283.

71. Lea, *King Ranch,* 353.

72. The marriage record is from State of Texas, County of Nueces, Rites of Matrimony between Louis Morris Welton and Miss Ella Morse King, 16th day of January, 1882, Records of Marriage, 171. The birth date of Henrietta Mary King Welton on July 7, 1882, in St. Louis, Missouri, is found at http://www.randolpharchives.org/genmod-cvs/pedigree.php?rootid=I32133&PEDIGREE_GENERATIONS=4&talloffset=1&ged=HR_PWC.ged.

73. Lea, *King Ranch,* 353–54.

74. Ibid., 354.

75. Savage, *For Life and Love,* 236.

76. Margaret Lasater Clark and the Historical Committee, *On This Bluff: Centennial History 1867–1967* (Corpus Christi: First Presbyterian Church), 110.

77. Ibid., 37.

78. *Corpus Christi Caller,* January 21, 1883.

79. Robert Justus Kleberg (Sr.), letter to Robert Justus Kleberg (I), Feb. 12, 1883, Box 2J51, Rudolph Kleberg Papers, Dolph Briscoe Center for American History, University of Texas at Austin.

80. Monday and Vick, *Petra's Legacy,* 296.

81. Ibid.

82. Ibid., 297.

83. Quoted in Lea, *King Ranch,* 355.

84. Monday and Vick, *Petra's Legacy,* 297.

85. Lea, *King Ranch,* 356.

86. Monday and Vick, *Petra's Legacy,* 298.

87. Ibid., 299.

88. *Corpus Christi Caller,* May 27, 1883.

89. Lea, *King Ranch,* 357.

90. Supreme Court of Texas No. 01–0430. Argued April 2, 2003. Decided August 28, 2003. Rehearing denied November 21, 2003. 118 SW. 3d 742. *King Ranch, Inc. v. Chapman,* 747, p. 3. http://demo.lawriter.net/states/TX/books/case_Law/result?number=1.

91. Monday and Vick, *Petra's Legacy,* 299–300.

92. Ibid.

93. Lea, *King Ranch,* 343.

94. Ibid., 358.

95. Mrs. Stayton, whom Robert called his "other mother," was the wife of John W. Stayton of Cuero. Kleberg read history and law in the office of John W. Stayton. Lea, *King Ranch,* 477.

96. Lea, *King Ranch,* 364.

97. Monday and Vick, *Petra's Legacy,* 300.

98. Ibid., 301.

99. *Corpus Christi Caller,* November 4, 1883.

100. All quoted in Lea, *King Ranch,* 359.

The Love Letters, 1884–1887

1. Tom Lea, *The King Ranch* (Boston: Little, Brown, 1957), 777n7. Collins Station, the mail center for ranchers between Corpus Christi and San Diego, was about five miles east of present-day Alice and was the mailing address for the ranch. The ranch's letterhead of that era carried the inscription "King's Rancho, Santa Gertrudis, Collins, Nueces County, Texas."

2. Dick Frost, *The King Ranch Papers: An Unauthorized and Irreverent History of the World's Largest Landholders; The Kleberg Family* (Chicago: Aquarius Rising Press, 1985), 77. "At home on the Santa Gertrudis with Papa was the obedient and attentive youngest daughter Alice. She kept Mama in St. Louis up to date on the news, put Papa to bed, and saw her beau Robert Kleberg." Ibid., 80. After Lee's death, Henrietta, her health broken, spent many months in St. Louis trying to recover from the loss while Alice tried to keep her ailing, grieving father from drinking.

3. Murphy Givens, "Martha Rabb, Cattle Queen of Texas," *Corpus Christi Caller-Times,* posted April 9, 2008, http://www.caller.com/news/2008/apr/09/martha-rabb-cattle-queen-of-texas/ (accessed January 17, 2010). See also Jane Clements Monday and Frances Brannen Vick, *Petra's Legacy: The South Texas Ranching Empire of Petra Vela and Mifflin Kenedy* (College Station: Texas A&M University Press, 2007), 192.

4. "Kleberg, Marcellus E.," *Handbook of Texas Online,* http://www.tshaonline.org/handbook/online/articles/KK/fk12.html (accessed March 15, 2010). Marcellus Kleberg graduated from the law school of Washington and Lee University in 1872, established a law practice in DeWitt County, Texas, in

1873, and was elected to the Thirteenth Texas Legislature, serving in the lower house. He moved to Bellville in 1875, formed a law partnership with B. T. Harris, and on October 24, 1875, married Emilie Miller of Austin. Later that year he moved his law practice to Galveston. In Galveston, Marcellus Kleberg served as city attorney, city commissioner, and as a trustee and president of the school board for eighteen years.

5. "Kleberg, Rosalie von Roeder," *Handbook of Texas Online,* http://www.tshaonline.org/handbook/online/articles/KK/fk112.html (accessed March 15, 2010). Rosalie von Roeder Kleberg, the daughter of Lt. Ludwig Siegismund Anton and Caroline Luise (Sack) von Roeder, was born July 20, 1813, at Vorden, Westphalia. She was probably reared at the family estate, Marienmünster, near Höxter, Westphalia, and her major occupations were playing the piano and doing fancy handwork. She met Robert Justus Kleberg I through her brother, who knew him from Georg August University, Göttingen. When the family's financial circumstances declined, they decided to immigrate to Texas. Rosalie agreed to marry Kleberg if he would also move to Texas. Their wedding took place on September 4, 1834. She was buried on the ranch of her daughter Caroline, who married Robert C. Eckhardt. See also Sons of DeWitt Colony Texas, "Robert Justus Kleberg," http://www.tamu.edu/ccbn/dewitt/kleberg.htm (accessed March 15, 2010).

6. "Kleberg, Rosalie von Roeder," *Handbook of Texas Online,* http://www.tshaonline.org/handbook/online/articles/KK/fk112.html (accessed March 15, 2010). See also Sons of DeWitt Colony Texas, "Robert Justus Kleberg."

7. *Fort Worth Daily Gazette,* December 11, 1883, http://chroniclingamerica.loc.gov/lccn/sn86064205/1883-12-11/ed-1/seq-2/;words=Stuttz+J+g+G+j (accessed January 25, 2010). The troupe also presented plays such as *Jack Sheppard, Lady Audley's Secret, The Two Orphans,* and *Camille.* Between acts, the troupe sang, did poetry recitations, and performed comedy routines. Such troupes traveled to the same towns year after year. The *Fort Worth Daily Gazette* announced on December 11, 1883, that the "great Stuttz combination, twenty-six in number, are playing tonight to a good house. Mr. J. G. Stuttz and E. Alma Stuttz . . . are rendering the *Two Orphans* tonight." In Corpus Christi, the troupe performed *The Silver King, Ten Nights in a Barroom,* and *Camille. Corpus Christi Caller,* May 18, 1884, http://chroniclingamerica.loc.gov/lccn/sn86064205/1883-12-11/ed-1/seq-2/;words=Stuttz+J+g+G+j (accessed January 25, 2010). According to the August 3, 1884, issue of the *Corpus Christi Caller,* "Mr. J. G. Stuttz dramatic company closed its summer performances Friday—left Sat. for Indianola—were here for 3 mo."

8. Robert's concern about Alice's health was well founded. According to South Texas scholar Bruce Cheeseman, "Yellow fever, caused by a virus, is transmitted among susceptible hosts by several species of mosquitos. For more than two hundred years, it was one of the great plagues of the world. The tropical and subtropical regions of the Americas were subjected to devastating epidemics, and serious outbreaks occurred as far north as Boston. . . . Epidemics repeatedly swept over the southern United States, decimating populations, paralyzing industry and trade, and holding the people of the South in a state of perpetual dread. . . . The last outbreak in the United States occurred in 1905, when New Orleans and other ports of the South were invaded." Maria von Blucher, *Maria von Blucher's Corpus Christi: Letters from the South Texas Frontier, 1849–1879,* ed. Bruce Cheeseman (College Station: Texas A&M University Press, 2002), 268n62. See also ibid., 88–89, for Maria von Blucher's description of her own bout with yellow fever.

9. Some nineteenth-century issues of the *Corpus Christi Caller* may be found in the Special Collections & Archives Department, Mary and Jeff Bell Library, Texas A&M University–Corpus Christi.

10. Monday and Vick, *Petra's Legacy,* 241–43. Sarah Josephine Kenedy had married Dr. Arthur E. Spohn on November 22, 1876. Sarah's father, Mifflin Kenedy, had married Petra Vela of Mier, Mexico, on April 16, 1852. Petra already had seven children from her previous alliance with Luis de Vidal, and Petra and Mifflin had six children of their own. See also "Kenedy, Mifflin," *Handbook of Texas Online,* http://www.tshaonline.org/handbook/online/articles/KK/fke23html (accessed March 20, 2010).

11. Murphy Givens, "City's Historic Hotels Date Back to the 1840s," *Corpus Christi Caller-Times,* August 26, 2009, http://www.caller.com/news/2009/aug/26/citys-historic-hotels-date-back-to-the-1840s/ (accessed January 17, 2010, March 17, 2010). After it opened, the St. James Hotel was sold to William Rogers, and William Biggio was hired to run it. John Nance Garner and Jim Hogg stayed there, as did gunmen John Wesley Hardin and Ben Thompson.

12. Headaches can be categorized as either primary or secondary; primary headaches include migraines, tension headaches, and cluster headaches. Secondary headaches are caused by disease. "Headache Updates," http://www.headacheupdates.com/migraine/migraine-headache/migraine-overview/stress-fatigue-cause-headaches-migraine.htm (accessed March 17, 2010).

13. Lea, *King Ranch,* 343. "Etta" was named Henrietta, for her grandmother. She was the only daughter of Ella and Louis Welton. Etta married Nathaniel Burwell Page of Virginia and later sold her interest in the eastern

sector of the Norias Division to Alice Kleberg for four dollars an acre and other consideration. She also assumed a share of the King estate debt. See Lea, *King Ranch,* 568.

14. Ursula Gerta McGraw, "Robert Justus Kleberg: Founding Father" (master's thesis, Texas A&I University, 1990), 58.

15. Lea, *King Ranch,* 442n80.

16. Ibid., 477, 498. See also ibid., 438, for the progression of the law firm: [Stephen] Powers and [Nestor] Maxam; Powers and [James B.] Wells; Wells and [Robert B.] Rentfro; Wells, Rentfro and [Benjamin O.] Hicks; Wells, [Robert W.] Stayton and [Robert J.] Kleberg; James B. Wells; Wells and [Joseph K.] Wells. In 1884, Stayton declined to run for Congress from the Seventh District, influenced to some degree by a petition from the Texas Bar Association, which pleaded that he not resign the bench. Several years later, when Justice Asa H. Willie resigned from the bench on March 3, 1888, Governor Lawrence Sullivan Ross promoted Stayton to chief justice, and voters elected him to a new six-year term in November. "Stayton, John William," *Handbook of Texas Online,* http://www.tshaonline.org/handbook/online/articles/SS/fst23.html (accessed March 29, 2010).

17. "University of Texas at Austin," *Handbook of Texas Online,* http://www.tshaonline.org/handbook/online/articles/UU/kcu9.html (accessed April 12, 2010).

18. Monday and Vick, *Petra's Legacy,* 291.

19. Lea, *King Ranch,* 323.

20. Regarding the "Laredo Excursionists," the *Corpus Christi Caller* reported on October 5, 1884, that an excursion to Corpus Christi from Saltillo would leave at 5 a.m. and arrive in Monterrey at 8:35 and then proceed to Laredo at 4:45 and Corpus Christi at 11:40 at night. The round trip was $5.75 in Mexican currency.

21. "Lovenskiold, Charles Crimus Thorkeli De," *Handbook of Texas Online,* http://www.tshaonline.org/handbook/online/articles/LL/fl033.html (accessed January 13, 2010). The *Corpus Christi Caller* of July 18, 1886, noted that "Miss Emelie R. Lovenskiold married Thomas B. Southgate by Rev. Father Jaillet in the residence of bride's mother. The bride, in magnificent costume, entered on the arm of Capt. M. Kenedy followed by Mr. U. Lott and others. Supper followed in adjoining room." See also *The Southwestern Reporter,* vol. 229 (West Publishing Company, 1921), 890.

22. "Doddridge, Perry," *Handbook of Texas Online,* http://www.tshaonline.org/handbook/online/articles/DD/fd042.html (accessed January 13, 2010). Doddridge opened a merchandising business in Corpus

Christi in 1865 under the name Manuel Bustamente and Company. He then purchased an exchange and commission business in 1868 with a partner, Allen M. Davis. Doddridge and Davis went on to establish the first bank in Corpus Christi in 1871. Davis sold out in 1885, leaving Doddridge and Company a sole proprietorship. Maria Blucher wrote to her parents that the Doddridges, "friends of ours, . . . are very, very rich and lost their only child, a boy of six or seven years, to yellow fever, and since that time they always travel in summer. . . . Every Thursday they have a party at their house, where old and young amuse themselves brilliantly and feast on the best fare. . . . Rachel Doddridge . . . has grown so fat." Von Blucher, *Maria von Blucher's Corpus Christi,* 203.

23. "Murphy, John Bernard," *Handbook of Texas Online,* http://www.tshaonline.org/handbook/online/articles/MM/fmu37.html (accessed January 13, 2010). Murphy's wife was the former Margaret Mary Healy. After moving to Corpus Christi, he had practiced law and managed his various business interests. At one time he served as district attorney for Nueces County.

24. "Kenedy, Mifflin," *Handbook of Texas Online,* http://www.tshaonline.org/handbook/online/articles/KK/fke23.html (accessed March 20, 2010). In 1860, Kenedy and King, the two riverboat captains, partnered once again in buying Rancho Santa Gertrudis. They later dissolved the partnership but meticulously divided the stock. Always interested in transportation, Kenedy entered the field of railroad construction in 1876 to help Uriah Lott build the Corpus Christi, San Diego and Rio Grande line from Corpus Christi to Laredo. In 1885, he supplied the money and credit for Lott to build seven hundred miles of the San Antonio and Aransas Pass Railway. See Monday and Vick, *Petra's Legacy,* for a complete history of the Kenedy family during Petra Kenedy's lifetime. At the time of Robert Kleberg's visit with him the day he wrote this letter, Captain Kenedy was apparently suffering from an irritation of the colon or small bowel. Charles Monday, M.D., from a discussion with the authors, May 11, 2010.

25. "Crazy quilting," http://en.wikipedia.org/wiki/Crazy_quilting (accessed April 12, 2010). To make crazy quilts, hobbyists used small and irregular-shaped pieces of fabric, including exotic fabrics such as velvet, satin, tulle, silk, or brocade, and heavy embellishments such as buttons, lace, ribbons, beads, or embroidery. Crazy quilting was very creative and free flowing by nature. The imagination and skill of the hobbyist was the only limit. These quilts were for decorative rather than utilitarian purposes and rarely had the internal batting found in regular quilts.

26. "George Lyttelton, 1st Baron Lyttelton" PC (1709–1773), http://

en.wikipedia.org/wiki/George_Lyttelton,_1st_Baron_Lyttelton (accessed May 6, 2010). Sir George Lyttelton was a British politician, statesman, and patron of the arts.

27. "Corpus Christi *Caller-Times*," *Handbook of Texas Online*, http://www.tshaonline.org/handbook/online/articles/CC/eec12.html (accessed May 16, 2010).

28. A. G. Heaney was a doctor in Corpus Christi for more than seventy years. His son, D. Heaney, was involved with the telephone company later and had the first telephone in the city. E-mail from Cecilia Venable, Texas A&M University–Corpus Christi, November 3, 2010, in possession of authors.

29. "United States Presidential Election, 1884," http://en.wikipedia.org/wiki/United_States_presidential_election,_1884 (accessed March 20, 2010).

30. "Kleberg, Rudolph," *Handbook of Texas Online*, http://www.tshaonline.org/handbook/online/articles/KK/fk17.html (accessed March 20, 2010).

31. Mike Cox, "Photographer Louis de Planque," Texas Tales column, February 1, 2007, http://www.texasescapes.com/MikeCoxTexasTales/Photographer-Louis-de-Planque.htm (accessed January 14, 2010). Cox notes that there is a well-written and researched chapter on de Planque and many of his photographs in Jerry Thompson and Lawrence T. Jones III, *Civil War and Revolution on the Rio Grande Frontier: A Narrative and Photographic History* (Austin: Texas State Historical Association, 2004). Cox also notes that in 1939 Bill Barnard wrote in the *Corpus Christi Caller-Times* that "no celebrity or near-celebrity ever visited . . . without being tracked down . . . and dragged off to [de Planque's] photo art studio. He was the only photographer in town and took thousands of pictures." Quoted in Cox, "Photographer Louis de Planque,"

32. Lea, *King Ranch*, 509.

33. Ibid., 478.

34. "Mammals of Texas," http://www.mammalsociety.org/statelists/txmammals.html (accessed March 22, 2010). Also see the *Corpus Christi Caller*, December 28, 1884, which mentions such a hunt: "Party of young folks left yesterday for the woods on a grand cat hunt."

35. According to the July 20, 1884, issue of the *Corpus Christi Caller*, "Col. Ford, Jno Greer, W. P. Caruthers left Wed. for a visit to Santa Gertrudis. [Captain King] has every comfort and convenience of modern life that money can get is at hand. You may tramp through Texas without a dollar in your pocket

with hardly a rag to your back and receive the treatment due a prince. This is not meant as an invitation to tramps.

"A ride in the evening in [a] comfortable coach with the Captain and his family across the prairies where the wild deer, and cattle graze is a pleasure long to be remembered. The breeze direct from the Gulf is cool and invigorating. The fine grass and fat cattle lend a charm to the picture that must be seen to be appreciated. While living in this ease there is no ostentation. One feels at home no matter how humble he has been. Such is the home of Capt. King and his estimable family."

36. McGraw, "Robert Justus Kleberg," 61.

37. "National Trail," *Handbook of Texas Online,* http://www.tshaonline.org/handbook/online/articles/NN/ayn1.html (accessed April 13, 2010). A bill to create the National Trail was finally introduced in the House of Representatives in 1886, but northern cattle interests and railroads wanting to replace cattle trails with rails managed to have the bill tabled in the House committee on commerce.

38. Lea, *King Ranch,* 343.

39. Monday and Vick, *Petra's Legacy,* 115.

40. Lea, *King Ranch,* 343.

41. William DeRyee possessed knowledge of various chemicals and natural resources, including metallic ores; his work in analyzing ore samples had earned him enough money to open a drugstore in Corpus Christi in January 1866. During the yellow fever epidemic of 1867, DeRyee began treating patients himself because all of the local physicians died in the epidemic. His treatment consisted of keeping the extremities warm with hot ashes, reducing the fever with cold towels and doses of potassium salicylate or salicin, and controlling convulsions with morphia. He was afterward known as "Dr." DeRyee. "Charley" likely refers to William DeRyee's son, Charles DeRyee, discoverer of the boll weevil in Texas. "DeRyee, William," *Handbook of Texas Online,* http://www.tshaonline.org/handbook/online/articles/DD/fde44.html (accessed May 30, 2010); "Howard Associations," *Handbook of Texas Online,* http://www.tshaonline.org/handbook/online/articles/HH/vwh1.html (accessed May 30, 2010).

42. E-mail from Cecilia Venable, November 3, 2010, in possession of authors.

43. "Establishment of the Myrtle Club," *Corpus Christi Caller-Times,* 1883–1983 Centennial Issue, http://www.cclibraries.com/local_history/laretama/lrhistory.htm#_ednref11 (accessed January 17, 2010). Some of the

membership included prominent businessmen and professionals such as David Hirsch, Thomas and James Hickey, George F. Evans, Dr. A. E. Spohn, John S. McCampbell, Atlee McCampbell, R. J. Kleberg Sr., Charles Weil, M. Lichtenstein, John Uehinger, Dr. T. S. Burke, Dr. Thomas J. Turpin, bookstore owner and alderman T. P. Rivera; banker and alderman Perry Doddridge; builder, architect, and alderman Charles Carroll; grocer and alderman George French; physician and photographer W. W. McGregor; merchant and grocer S. W. Rankin; and attorney G. R. Scott. Thomas S. Southgate was instrumental in getting the club started. In 1884, the club began to have "Ladies Day," allowing women to enter the premises for four days out of each month.

44. Lea, *King Ranch,* 366. See also Monday and Vick, *Petra's Legacy,* 332.

45. Lea, *King Ranch,* 466n41.

46. Ibid., 361.

47. Margaret Lasater Clark and the Historical Committee, *On This Bluff: Centennial History 1867-1967* (Corpus Christi: First Presbyterian Church, 1967), 38.

48. Quoted in Lea, *King Ranch,* 366.

49. Lea, *King Ranch,* 368.

50. Mifflin Kenedy, letter dated March 26, 1885, to Mrs. H. M. King, Menger Hotel, San Antonio, in possession of Bruce Cheeseman, copy given to Jane Clements Monday.

51. Ibid.

52. Cameron County (Tex.), County Surveyor, http://lib3.utpa.edu/search~S5?/aCameron+County+%28Tex.%29.+County+Surveyor./acameron+county+tex+county+surveyor/-3,-1,0,B/browse (accessed March 27, 2010); Lea, *King Ranch,* 472.

53. Monday and Vick, *Petra's Legacy,* 220, 260.

54. Lea, *King Ranch,* 368.

55. Ibid., 369.

56. *San Antonio Express,* April 16, 1885, Special Collections and Archives, Mary and Jeff Bell Library, Texas A&M University–Corpus Christi.

57. *Corpus Christi Caller,* April 26, 1885.

58. Captain King quoted in Lea, *King Ranch,* 470.

59. Lea, *King Ranch,* 471.

60. Ibid., 473.

61. "General Charles King Tribute Site," http://www.erbzine.com/mag12/1268.html (accessed March 25, 2010). See also "Guide to the Charles King Archival Collection," http://www.kenosha.org/civilwar/documents/

CharlesKingCollection.pdf (accessed March 25, 2010). Charles King was born October 12, 1844, in Albany, New York, and died March 17, 1933, in Milwaukee. His most popular writings were *Campaigning with Crook, The Colonel's Daughter* (Philadelphia: J. B. Lippincott, 1882), *Daughter of the Sioux, Fort Frayne,* and *Under Fire.* Almost all his writings revolved around the US Army and his involvement in the Civil War, Indian Wars, and the Spanish-American War. He is often credited with founding the Western genre.

62. "University of Virginia Library, Catalogue of the Officers and Students of the University of Virginia," http://xtf.lib.virginia.edu/xtf/view?docId=2005_Q4_3/uvaBook/tei/z000000184.xml;chunk.id=d14;toc.depth=1;toc.id=d14;brand=default (accessed January 27, 2010).

63. "Wells, James Babbage, Jr.," *Handbook of Texas Online,* http://www.tshaonline.org/handbook/online/articles/WW/fwe22.html (accessed January 13, 2010). By the time of Powers's death in 1882, Wells had emerged as his chief lieutenant and heir apparent.

64. Monday and Vick, *Petra's Legacy,* 348–49.

65. Ibid., 353–54.

66. "Ingleside, Texas," *Handbook of Texas Online,* http://www.tshaonline.org/handbook/online/articles/II/hfi1.html (accessed March 26, 2010). Ingleside had its origins in 1854, when settler George C. Hatch purchased land on both sides of a bayou and then resold acreage to other settlers, who built homes on the bayou and at Ingleside Cove. Steamships plied the waters between Corpus Christi and Ingleside, carrying trade goods and stopping at Indianola.

67. "Fulton, George Ware, Jr.," *Handbook of Texas Online,* http://www.tshaonline.org/handbook/online/articles/FF/ffu9.html (accessed January 13, 2010). The Coleman-Fulton Pasture Company was formed in 1879 after financial and personal problems led to the dissolution of a larger ranching concern founded in 1871. Colonel George Ware Fulton, head of the company, brought his son G. W. Fulton Jr. into the firm in 1884, and the younger man replaced Tom Coleman as ranch superintendent in 1885.

68. Lea, *King Ranch,* 482.

69. See Monday and Vick, *Petra's Legacy,* 351–56, for a full discussion of how the estate was handled.

70. Lea, *King Ranch,* 496.

71. Ibid., 472, 781n16.

72. "Holbein, Reuben," *Handbook of Texas Online,* http://www.tshaonline.org/handbook/online/articles/HH/fhoaz.html (accessed March 26, 2010).

73. Lea, *King Ranch,* 307–308. John Fitch had been a captain in the Confederate Army under Colonel John S. Ford. He also served in the Texas Rangers under Captain Bill Tobin and did considerable fighting in the expedition to hunt down the populist Mexican outlaw Juan Cortina, who had been staging attacks against American targets along on the Rio Grande. See http://www.cclibraries.com/local_history/oldbayview/fitchjwobituary.htm (accessed March 31, 2010).

74. Lea, *King Ranch,* 242.

75. "Yturria, Francisco," *Handbook of Texas Online,* http://www.tshaonline.org/handbook/online/articles/YY/fyt1.html (accessed March 26, 2010). See also http://blue.utb.edu/hunter/yturria/gallery.shtml.

76. Lea, *King Ranch,* 339.

77. Ibid., 482.

78. Ibid., 103.

79. Jessica Brannon-Wranosky, *Corpus Christi History before La Retama,* 2004, http://www.cclibraries.com/local_history/laretama/lrhistory.htm#_ednref11 (accessed January 17, 2010).

80. J. C. Friedrich von Schiller, *Literary and Philosophical Essays* (New York: P. F. Collier & Son, 1909–1914). His works often focused on concepts of beauty, goodness, and human freedom. See http://en.wikipedia.org/wiki/Friedrich_Schiller (accessed March 27, 2010).

81. "Establishment of the Myrtle Club," *Corpus Christi Caller-Times* 1883–1983 Centennial Issue.

82. E-mail from Cecilia Venable, November 3, 2010, in possession of authors.

83. "Biography of Emma Abbott," http://www.alliancelibrarysystem.com/IllinoisWomen/files/pe/html/peabj.html (accessed January 27, 2010). This "opera in three acts by Donizetti, words by Rossi, takes place in 1760 during the reign of Louis XV at Chamounix and Paris." "*Linda di Chamounix,* by Gaetano Donizetti," http://www.musicwithease.com/donizetti-linda-chamounix.html (accessed January 25, 2010). Emma Abbott organized the Abbott English Opera Company, which toured extensively for thirteen years in the northern, northwestern, and southern regions of the United States. In 1884 Abbott appeared at the Metropolitan Opera in New York to great acclaim. "Biography of Emma Abbott." For a photograph of Emma Abbott playing Linda in the opera *Linda de Chamounix,* see the print by photographer Tomlinson of Detroit at http://www.historicopera.com/p-usa-page1.html (accessed January 27, 2010).

84. "Turner, Ezekiel B.," *Handbook of Texas Online,* http://www

.tshaonline.org/handbook/online/articles/TT/ftu10.html (accessed January 13, 2010). An outspoken Unionist, Turner left Texas, probably in 1862, and returned with the federal forces that occupied Brownsville in November 1863. He received an appointment from Andrew J. Hamilton, President Lincoln's military governor of Texas, as prosecuting attorney of the provisional court established in that city, and his Unionism led to numerous appointments during Reconstruction. In 1880 President Rutherford B. Hayes appointed Turner judge of the Western Judicial District of Texas. In that position he was the first federal judge to rule that the Civil Rights Act of 1875 was unconstitutional, and it was struck down by the Supreme Court in 1883. Turner remained a federal judge until his death on June 2, 1888.

85. Opera houses, even in smaller communities, were venues for a variety of performances. In Texas, many settlers (particularly German immigrants) were well acquainted with opera. Theatricals were the most common types of performance, however. For many communities, itinerant dramatic troupes were the only sources of entertainment. Charles Brown Hagemeier, "The Lubbock Opera House—A Study in Associationism" (master's thesis, Texas Tech University, 1990), http://etd.lib.ttu.edu/theses/available/etd-08272008-31295010064680/unrestricted/31295010064680.pdf (accessed January 27, 2010).

86. Mourning stationery consisted of writing papers and envelopes with a black border, and it was meant to be used by the deceased's family during the customary twelve-month period of mourning. Captain King had died in April 1885, so this stationery was likely used because the family was still observing the period of mourning for him. "Mourning Stationary [*sic*]," http://www.riversideca.gov/museum/hh-virtual/alcovemore.htm (accessed April 26, 2010).

87. Annie S. Swan, *Marion Forsyth: or Unspotted from the World* (Edinburgh: Oliphant, Anderson & Ferrier, 1883), 56–57. Annie Shepherd Swan was a popular writer of romantic fiction for young women during the Victorian period. She wrote more than two hundred novels, serials, short stories, and other works, including poetry, from 1878 until her death in 1943. She was one of the first to contribute to women's magazines. Her breakout novel, *Aldersyde,* was published in 1883, at the time this poem was written. She later became a well-known suffragist and was also involved in the Temperance movement in Britain. However, at the time this poem was written, in 1883, her works were described as featuring themes of "sisterly and motherly love, the virtues of a good woman, and a happy resolution of romantic problems." "Annie S. Swan," http://en.wikipedia.org/wiki/Annie_Shepherd_Swan (ac-

cessed April 24, 2010). See also Moira Burgess, "Annie S. Swan," *Discovering Scottish Writers,* ed. Alan Reid and Brian D. Osborne (Hamilton and Edinburgh: Scottish Library Association, 1997); and John Sutherland, *The Stanford Companion to Victorian Fiction* (Stanford, Calif.: Stanford University Press, 1990), 200–201, http://orlando.cambridge.org/public/svPeople?person_id=swana2 (accessed April 24, 2010).

88. Helen Kleberg Groves, *Bob and Helen Kleberg of King Ranch* (Albany, Tex.: Bright Sky Press, 2004), 21.

89. *Corpus Christi Caller,* August 12, 1883.

90. During this period, Gulf Coast commercial interests wanted a deep water Gulf port. Galveston was always the first possible site mentioned for the construction and development of a deep water port, but Aransas Pass also entered the competition. By 1887, Uriah Lott, the business community of Corpus Christi, and the developers of Aransas Pass and local harbors were ready for deep water and their share of congressional attention. Lott invited Galvestonians to Aransas Pass in the hope that Congress would designate two Gulf Coast sites for deep water port development. Earle B. Young, *Galveston and the Great West* (College Station: Texas A&M University Press, 1997), 131, 133, 135–36.

91. Graham, *Kings of Texas,* 196.

92. Lea, *King Ranch,* 482.

93. Quoted in ibid., 481.

94. Ibid., 474.

95. Groves, *Bob and Helen Kleberg,* 21.

96. Quoted in Lea, *King Ranch,* 481.

97. Monday and Vick, *Petra's Legacy,* 332.

98. "Lott, Uriah," *Handbook of Texas Online,* http://www.tshaonline.org/handbook/online/articles/LL/fl024.html (accessed January 17, 2010). Lott played a significant role in developing transportation in the Corpus Christi and Rio Grande Valley areas as well as in South Texas generally. See also Monday and Vick, *Petra's Legacy,* 234, 244, 264.

99. Lea, *King Ranch,* 606. Robert Driscoll began a ranching career and accumulated vast holdings that covered several counties. In *A Vaquero of the Brush Country* (1929), J. Frank Dobie wrote that "Robert Driscoll, although among the younger men of the outfit, was unanimously chosen as boss, and no better choice could have been made. He was not only an expert vaquero and genuine cowman, but also a good manager." Quoted at http://www.dosvaqueros.com/history.html (accessed April 7, 2010).

The Driscolls were from a pioneer family. Daniel O'Driscoll, father of

Robert, fought at San Jacinto and afterward settled around Refugio, where he became a county official. Clara's father Robert and his brother Jeremiah fought in the Civil War. After the war they began to add land and cattle to what their father had left them. Before Clara was ten, Robert had bought the Palo Alto Ranch in Nueces County, twenty-two miles from Corpus Christi, near present-day Driscoll. Young Clara grew up at Palo Alto Ranch, where one of the family's favorite activities was a South Texas version of foxhunting, with coyotes taking the place of foxes. Later in her life, Clara Driscoll saved the Alamo from being renovated for commercial use and was an author, politician, banker, and cattlewoman who was at home in elite social circles in New York. Corpus Christi got its naval air station in large part due to her political influence with President Franklin D. Roosevelt and the Democratic Party. Murphy Givens, "Corpus Christi History," *Corpus Christi Caller-Times,* May 16, 2001, http://www.caller2.com/2001/may/16/today/murphygi/176.html (accessed April 7, 2010).

100. Graham, *Kings of Texas,* 144.

101. Mona D. Sizer, *The King Ranch Story* (Dallas: Republic of Texas Press, 1999), 145.

102. *Corpus Christi Caller,* November 28, 1886.

103. *Corpus Christi Caller,* December 11, 1887.

104. Lea, *King Ranch,* 485–87.

105. Ibid., 499.

106. Ibid., 496.

107. Hugh Best, *Debrett's Texas Peerage* (New York: Coward-McCann, 1983), 55.

108. "Finlay, George P.," *Handbook of Texas Online,* http://www.tshaonline.org/handbook/online/articles/FF/ffi11.html (accessed January 14, 2010).

109. "John Hancock," http://en.wikipedia.org/wiki/John_Hancock_(Texas_politician) (accessed April 7, 2010). See also http://www.nytimes.com/1865/08/02/news/texas-judge-hancock-declines-a-nomination-for-governor.html?pagewanted=1 (accessed April 7, 2010).

110. Alice King Kleberg's letter to "My Darling" was written on beautifully engraved stationery with her monogram; a copy of it was given to Jane Clements Monday by Bruce Cheeseman.

111. Lea, *King Ranch,* 526.

112. Groves, *Bob and Helen Kleberg,* 12.

113. Lea, *King Ranch,* 631.

114. "Collins, Texas (Nueces County)," *Handbook of Texas Online,* http://www.tshaonline.org/handbook/online/articles/hvc63 (accessed Au-

gust 4, 2011). See also Jean Darby, *Alice: A Centennial History, 1888–1988* (San Antonio: Marion Koogler McNay Art Museum, 1992). In the late 1880s Phil Hobbs would travel in a horse-drawn wagon from Collins to the town of Kleberg to pick up the mail at the intersection of the San Antonio and Aransas Pass and the Texas-Mexican railways. He then returned to Collins, and people living in Kleberg had to go to Collins for the mail. The Collins post office was closed permanently on February 26, 1892.

115. Lea, *King Ranch*, 361–62.

Epilogue, 1887–2011

1. See Robert Kleberg's love letter of July 27, 1887, for reference to his search for temporary accommodations in town. See also Tom Lea, *The King Ranch* (Boston: Little, Brown, 1957), 508.

2. Lea, *King Ranch*, 508.

3. Robert Kleberg, letter to Rudolph Kleberg, November 27, 1887, Box 2751, Rudolph Kleberg Papers, Dolph Briscoe Center for American History, University of Texas at Austin.

4. Helen Kleberg Groves, *Bob and Helen Kleberg of King Ranch* (Albany, Tex.: Bright Sky Press, 2004), 4.

5. E'Lane Carlisle Murray, "Recollections of Minerva King Patch," given to Bruce Cheeseman, March 1993, copy given to Jane Clements Monday, 3–4.

6. Lea, *King Ranch*, 521.

7. Ibid., 512.

8. Groves, *Bob and Helen Kleberg*, 186.

9. Lea, *King Ranch*, 508.

10. Ibid., 511.

11. Groves, *Bob and Helen Kleberg*, 21.

12. Lea, *King Ranch*, 522–23.

13. Murphy Givens, "Corpus Christi History—Storybook Mansions," June 27, 2001, http://www.caller2.com/2001/June/27/today/murphygi/3832.html (accessed January 17, 2010).

14. Dick Frost, *King Ranch Papers: An Unauthorized and Irreverent History of the World's Largest Landholders; The Kleberg Family* (Chicago: Aquarius Rising Press, 1985), 605.

15. Murray, "Recollections of Minerva King Patch," 5.

16. Lea, *King Ranch*, 498.

17. Frost, *King Ranch Papers*, 702.

18. Lea, *King Ranch,* 499–501.

19. Ibid., 504.

20. Ibid., 506.

21. Benjamin Franklin Yoakum (1859–1929) was an important railroad executive, and the town of Yoakum, Texas, was named for him. He was a manager of the San Antonio and Aransas Pass Railway, then of the Gulf, Colorado, and Santa Fe line, and finally of the Frisco (St. Louis and San Francisco Railway Company). Under his leadership the Frisco lines grew from twelve hundred to six thousand miles. In 1905 the Frisco and Rock Island lines were joined, and Yoakum became chairman of the combined company's executive committee. At the time, the Yoakum Line, as it was known, was the largest railroad system under individual control. "Yoakum, Benjamin Franklin," *Handbook of Texas Online,* http://www.tshaonline.org/handbook/online/articles/YY/fy01.html (accessed June 30, 2010).

22. Lea, *King Ranch,* 541.

23. Ibid., 542.

24. Quoted in ibid., 544.

25. Members of the Kleberg County Historical Commission and Other Volunteers, *Kleberg County Texas: A Collection of Historical Sketches and Family Histories* (N.p.: American Revolution Bicentennial Heritage Project, 1976), 173–75.

26. Lea, *King Ranch,* 533.

27. "J. A. van Blerk 'Met President Reitz deur Texas,'" trans. Natalie Alice van Blerk, ed. Martin Staples Shockley and A. Ray Stephens, *Southwestern Historical Quarterly* 74, no. 1 (July 1970): 91–92, http://texashistory.unt.edu/ark:/67531/metapth101200/m1/93/?q=J.%20A.%20van%20Blerk (accessed August 2, 2010).

28. Lea, *King Ranch,* 569–73 (quote, 571).

29. Ibid., 539.

30. Ibid., 629.

31. *Corpus Christi 100 Years* (Corpus Christi: Corpus Christi Caller-Times, 1952), 139.

32. Richard Harding Davis, *The West from a Car-Window* (New York: Harper & Brothers, 1892), 122.

33. Quoted in C. L. Douglas, *Cattle Kings of Texas* (Fort Worth: Branch-Smith, 1989), 95.

34. Don Graham, *Kings of Texas: The 150-Year Saga of an American Ranching Empire* (Hoboken, N.J.: John Wiley & Sons, 2003), 195.

35. Lea, *King Ranch,* 602–4.

36. Douglas, *Cattle Kings of Texas,* 91.

37. Graham, *Kings of Texas,* 204.

38. Lea, *King Ranch,* 624.

39. Ibid., 627.

40. Helen Kleberg Groves, *Bob and Helen Kleberg of King Ranch* (Albany, Tex.: Bright Sky Press, 2004), 21.

41. Quoted in ibid.

42. Lea, *King Ranch,* 592.

43. Caesar Kleberg was the son of Mathilde (Eckhardt) and Rudolph Kleberg, Robert Sr.'s brother. He was born September 20, 1873, at Cuero, Texas. After attending St. Edward's University in Austin, Caesar went to Washington, D.C., where he served on the staff of his father, who was a member of Congress from 1897 to 1903. He moved to the King Ranch in 1900 to begin work as chief assistant to his uncle, Robert J. Kleberg. "Kleberg, Caesar," *Handbook of Texas Online,* http://tshaonline.org/handbook/online/articles/fk116 (accessed August 8, 2011). When Caesar first lived and worked on the ranch, he was placed under the tutelage of Sam Ragland, the veteran superintendent of the Santa Gertrudis who was much respected for his knowledge of livestock and men. Both of these men were bachelors and lived in separate quarters rather than in the big ranch house. When Robert and Alice's boys Dick and Bob were old enough, they were moved to the bachelor quarters to live with the "bluff old bachelor" Sam Ragland. *Life,* July 15, 1957, digitized at Google Books (accessed August 8, 2011).

44. Lea, *King Ranch,* 622.

45. *Corpus Christi 100 Years,* 142.

46. John Cypher, *Bob Kleberg and the King Ranch—A Worldwide Sea of Grass* (Austin: University of Texas Press, 1995), vii.

47. Lea, *King Ranch,* 665.

48. Quoted in S. C. Gwynne, "The Next Frontier," *Texas Monthly,* August 1, 2007, http://www.texasmonthly.com/2007-08-01/feature.php (accessed July 22, 2009).

49. Quoted in Groves, *Bob and Helen Kleberg,* 21.

Bibliography

Becker, John T. "Jack." "J. P. Morris and the Rafter-3 Ranch." MA thesis, Texas Tech University, 2001.

Best, Hugh. *Debrett's Texas Peerage.* New York: Coward-McCann, 1983.

"Biography of Emma Abbott." http://www.alliancelibrarysystem.com/IllinoisWomen/files/pe/html/peabj.html (accessed January 27, 2010).

Brannon-Wranosky, Jessica. *Corpus Christi History before La Retama.* 2004. http://www.cclibraries.com/local_history/laretama/lrhistory.htm#_ednref11 (accessed January 17, 2010).

Brown, John Henry. "Robert Justus Kleberg." In *The Indian Wars and Pioneers of Texas,* 289–94. Austin: L. E. Daniell, 189?

Burgess, Moira. "Annie S. Swan." *Discovering Scottish Writers,* edited by Alan Reid and Brian D. Osborne. Hamilton and Edinburgh: Scottish Library Association, 1997.

Cameron County (Tex.). County Surveyor. http://lib3.utpa.edu/search~S5?/aCameron+County+%28Tex.%29.+County+Surveyor./acameron+county+tex+county+surveyor/-3,-1,0,B/browse (accessed March 27, 2010).

Cheeseman, Bruce. *Perfectly Exhausted with Pleasure.* Austin: Book Club of Texas, 1992.

Clark, Margaret Lasater, and the Historical Committee. *On This Bluff: Centennial History 1867–1967.* Corpus Christi: First Presbyterian Church, 1967.

Coker, Caleb, ed. *News from Brownsville: Helen Chapman's Letters from the Texas Military Frontier, 1848–1852.* Austin: Texas State Historical Association, 1992.

Corpus Christi 100 Years. Corpus Christi: Corpus Christi Caller-Times, 1952.

"Corpus Christi *Caller-Times.*" *Handbook of Texas Online.* http://www.tshaonline.org/handbook/online/articles/CC/eec12.html (accessed May 16, 2010).

Corpus Christi Caller-Times. Special Collections and Archives, Mary and Jeff Bell Library, Texas A&M University–Corpus Christi.

Cox, Mike. "Louis de Planque." Texas Tales column, February 1, 2007. http://www.texasescapes.com/MikeCoxTexasTales/Photographer-Louis-de-Planque.htm (accessed January 14, 2010).

Cypher, John. *Bob Kleberg and the King Ranch—A Worldwide Sea of Grass.* Austin: University of Texas Press, 1995.

Dacus, Joseph A., and James William Buel. *A Tour of St. Louis: or, The Inside Life of a Great City.* St. Louis: Western Publishing, 1878. Digitized by Google Books. http://books.google.com.

Davis, Richard Harding. *The West from a Car-Window.* New York: Harper & Brothers Publishers, 1892.

Dawson, Joseph Martin. "The Greatest Ranch in the World." *Texas Monthly* 3, no. 6 (April 1929): 463–70.

"DeRyee, William." *Handbook of Texas Online.* http://www.tshaonline.org/handbook/online/articles/DD/fde44.html (accessed May 30, 2010).

DeWitt County Historical Commission. *The History of DeWitt County.* Dallas: Curtis Media, 1991.

Dobie, J. Frank. *A Vaquero of the Brush Country.* Dallas: Southwest Press, 1929.

"Doddridge, Perry." *Handbook of Texas Online.* http://www.tshaonline.org/handbook/online/articles/DD/fd042.html (accessed January 13, 2010).

Douglas, C. L. *Cattle Kings of Texas.* Fort Worth: Branch-Smith, 1989.

"Establishment of the Myrtle Club," *Corpus Christi Caller,* 1883–1983 Centennial Issue. Special Collections and Archives, Mary and Jeff Bell Library, Texas A&M University–Corpus Christi Library.

"Finlay, George P." *Handbook of Texas Online.* http://www.tshaonline.org/handbook/online/articles/FF/ffi11.html (accessed January 14, 2010).

"Fitch, Capt. John." http://www.cclibraries.com/local_history/oldbayview/fitchjwobituary.htm (accessed March 31, 2010).

Ford, John Salmon. *Rip Ford's Texas,* edited by Stephen Oates. Austin: University of Texas Press, 1963.

Frost, Dick. *The King Ranch Papers: An Unauthorized and Irreverent History of the World's Largest Landholders; The Kleberg Family.* Chicago: Aquarius Rising Press, 1985.

"Fulton, George Ware, Jr." *Handbook of Texas Online.* http://www.tshaonline.org/handbook/online/articles/FF/ffu9.html (accessed January 13, 2010).

Givens, Murphy. "City's Historic Hotels Date Back to the 1840s." *Corpus*

Christi Caller-Times, August 26, 2009. http://www.caller.com/news/2009/aug/26/citys-historic-hotels-date-back-to-the-1840s/ (accessed January 17, 2010, March 17, 2010).

———. "Corpus Christi History." *Corpus Christi Caller-Times,* May 16, 2001. http://www.caller2.com/2001/may/16/today/murphygi/176.html (accessed April 7, 2010).

———. "Corpus Christi History—Storybook Mansions." *Corpus Christi Caller-Times,* June 27, 2001. http://www.caller2.com/2001/June/27/today/murphygi/3832.html (accessed January 17, 2010).

———. "Martha Rabb, Cattle Queen of Texas." *Corpus Christi Caller-Times,* April 9, 2008. http://www.caller.com/news/2008/apr/09/martha-rabb-cattle-queen-of-texas/ (accessed January 17, 2010).

Graham, Don. *Kings of Texas: The 150-Year Saga of an American Ranching Empire.* Hoboken, N.J.: John Wiley & Sons, 2003.

Groves, Helen Kleberg. *Bob and Helen Kleberg of King Ranch.* Albany, Tex.: Bright Sky Press, 2004.

"Guide to the Charles King Archival Collection." http://www.kenosha.org/civilwar/documents/CharlesKingCollection.pdf (accessed March 25, 2010).

Gwynne, S. C. "The Next Frontier." *Texas Monthly,* August 1, 2007. http://www.texasmonthly.com/2007-08-01/feature.php (accessed July 22, 2009).

Hagemeier, Charles Brown. "The Lubbock Opera House—A Study in Associationism." Master's thesis, Texas Tech University, 1990. http://etd.lib.ttu.edu/theses/available/etd-08272008-31295010064680/unrestricted/31295010064680.pdf (accessed January 27, 2010).

"Headache Updates." http://www.headacheupdates.com/migraine/migraine-headache/migraine-overview/stress-fatigue-cause-headaches-migraine.htm (accessed March 17, 2010).

"Holbein, Reuben." *Handbook of Texas Online.* http://www.tshaonline.org/handbook/online/articles/HH/fhoaz.html (accessed March 26, 2010).

"Howard Associations." *Handbook of Texas Online.* http://www.tshaonline.org/handbook/online/articles/HH/vwh1.html (accessed May 30, 2010).

"Ingleside, Texas." *Handbook of Texas Online.* http://www.tshaonline.org/handbook/online/articles/II/hfi1.html (accessed March 26, 2010).

"Kenedy, Mifflin." *Handbook of Texas Online.* http://www.tshaonline.org/handbook/online/articles/KK/fke23.html (accessed March 20, 2010).

King, General Charles. *The Colonel's Daughter, or, Winning His Spurs.* Philadelphia: J. B. Lippincott, 1882.

"King, General Charles, Tribute Site." http://www.erbzine.com/mag12/1268.html (accessed March 25, 2010).

King Ranch, Inc. v. Chapman. 118S.W.3d 742.

"Kleberg, Marcellus E." *Handbook of Texas Online.* http://www.tshaonline.org/handbook/online/articles/KK/fk12.html (accessed March 15, 2010).

Kleberg, Robert. Family Papers. Box 2J52. Dolph Briscoe Center for American History, University of Texas at Austin.

Kleberg, Robert J. Letter to his parents, July 24, 1881. Special Collections and Archives, Mary and Jeff Bell Library, Texas A&M University–Corpus Christi.

"Kleberg, Rosalie von Roeder." *Handbook of Texas Online.* http://www.tshaonline.org/handbook/online/articles/KK/fk112.html (accessed March 15, 2010).

"Kleberg, Rudolph." *Handbook of Texas Online.* http://www.tshaonline.org/handbook/online/articles/KK/fk17.html (accessed March 20, 2010).

Kleberg, Rudolph. Papers. Box 2751. Dolph Briscoe Center for American History, University of Texas at Austin.

Lea, Tom. *The King Ranch.* Boston: Little, Brown, 1957.

"*Linda di Chamounix,* by Gaetano Donizetti." http://www.musicwithease.com/donizetti-linda-chamounix.html (accessed January 27, 2010).

"Lott, Uriah." *Handbook of Texas Online.* http://www.tshaonline.org/handbook/online/articles/LL/fl024.html (accessed January 17, 2010).

"Lovenskiold, Charles Crimus Thorkeli De." *Handbook of Texas Online.* http://www.tshaonline.org/handbook/online/articles/LL/fl033.html (accessed January 13, 2010).

"Mammals of Texas." http://www.mammalsociety.org/statelists/txmammals.html (accessed March 22, 2010).

McGraw, Ursula Gerta. "Robert Justus Kleberg: Founding Father." Master's thesis, Texas A&I University, 1990.

Members of the Kleberg County Historical Commission and Other Volunteers. *Kleberg County Texas: A Collection of Historical Sketches and Family Histories.* American Revolution Bicentennial Heritage Project, 1976.

Monday, Jane Clements, and Frances Brannen Vick. *Petra's Legacy: The South Texas Ranching Empire of Petra Vela and Mifflin Kenedy.* College Station: Texas A&M University Press, 2007.

"Mourning Stationary [*sic*]." http://www.riversideca.gov/museum/hh-virtual/alcovemore.htm (accessed April 26, 2010).

"Murphy, John Bernard." *Handbook of Texas Online.* http://www.tshaonline

.org/handbook/online/articles/MM/fmu37.html (accessed January 13, 2010).

Murray, E'Lane Carlisle. Letter to Bruce Cheeseman, provided to Jane Clements Monday, including material from interview with Minerva King Patch.

———. "Recollections of Minerva King Patch," given to Bruce Cheeseman, 1993, provided to Jane Clements Monday.

"National Trail." *Handbook of Texas Online*. http://www.tshaonline.org/handbook/online/articles/NN/ayn1.html (accessed April 13, 2010).

San Antonio Express, April 16, 1885. Special Collections and Archives, Mary and Jeff Bell Library, Texas A&M University–Corpus Christi.

Savage, Henry. *For Life and Love*. New York: Rand McNally, 1893.

Schiller, J. C. Friedrich von. *Literary and Philosophical Essays*. New York: P. F. Collier, 1909–1914.

Sizer, Mona D. *The King Ranch Story: Truth and Myth*. Dallas: Republic of Texas Press, 1999.

Sons of DeWitt Colony Texas. "Robert Justus Kleberg." http://www.tamu.edu/ccbn/dewitt/kleberg.htm (accessed March 15, 2010).

The Southwestern Reporter. Vol. 229. N.p.: West Publishing Company, 1921.

Stambaugh, J. Lee, and Lillian J. Stambaugh. *The Lower Rio Grande Valley of Texas*. San Antonio: Naylor, 1954.

State of Texas. County of Nueces. Rites of Matrimony between Louis Morris Welton and Miss Ella Morse King, 16th day of January, 1882. Records of Marriage, 171.

Stayton, John William." *Handbook of Texas Online*. http://www.tshaonline.org/handbook/online/articles/SS/fst23.html (accessed March 29, 2010).

Stayton, Robert W. Letter to Hon. John A. Mobley, Welder Leshin LLP, Corpus Christi, Tex., December 16, 1957. Shared with authors on January 20, 2010.

Sutherland, John. *The Stanford Companion to Victorian Fiction*. Stanford, Calif.: Stanford University Press, 1990. http://orlando.cambridge.org/public/svPeople?person_id=swana2 (accessed April 26, 2010).

Thompson, Jerry, and Lawrence T. Jones III. *Civil War and Revolution on the Rio Grande Frontier: A Narrative and Photographic History*. Austin: Texas State Historical Association, 2004.

"Turner, Ezekiel B." *Handbook of Texas Online*. http://www.tshaonline.org/handbook/online/articles/TT/ftu10.html (accessed January 13, 2010).

"University of Texas at Austin." *Handbook of Texas Online*. http://www

.tshaonline.org/handbook/online/articles/UU/kcu9.html (accessed April 12, 2010).

"University of Virginia Library, Catalogue of the Officers and Students of the University of Virginia." http://xtf.lib.virginia.edu/xtf/view?docId=2005_Q4_3/uvaBook/tei/z000000184.xml;chunk.id=d14;toc.depth=1;toc.id=d14;brand=default (accessed January 27, 2010).

"van Blerk, J. A. 'Met President Reitz deur Texas.'" Translated by Natalie Alice van Blerk, edited by Martin Staples Shockley and A. Ray Stephens. *Southwestern Historical Quarterly* 74, no. 1 (July 1970): 81–98 available at http://texashistory.unt.edu/ark:/67531/metapth101200/m1/93/?q=J.%20A.%20van%20Blerk (accessed August 2, 2010). Kelly, Hubert. "America's Forbidden Kingdom." *Readers Digest,* May 1938.

von Blucher, Maria. *Maria von Blucher's Corpus Christi: Letters from the South Texas Frontier, 1849–1879,* edited by Bruce Cheeseman. College Station: Texas A&M University Press, 2002.

"Wells, James Babbage, Jr." *Handbook of Texas Online.* http://www.tshaonline.org/handbook/online/articles/WW/fwe22.html (accessed January 13, 2010).

"The World's Biggest Ranch." *Fortune,* December 1933, 48–109.

"Yoakum, Benjamin Franklin." *Handbook of Texas Online.* http://www.tshaonline.org/handbook/online/articles/YY/fy01.html (accessed June 30, 2010).

Young, Earle B. *Galveston and the Great West.* College Station: Texas A&M University Press, 1997.

"Yturria, Francisco." *Handbook of Texas Online.* http://www.tshaonline.org/handbook/online/articles/YY/fyt1.html (accessed March 26, 2010).

Index

Page numbers in *italics* refer to photographs.

Other titles in the Gulf Coast Books series:

Lighthouses of Texas / Baker and Holland
The Laguna Madre of Texas and Tamaulipas / Tunnell and Judd
Life on Matagorda Island / McAlister and McAlister
The Book of Texas Bays / Blackburn and Olive
Plants of the Texas Coastal Bend / Lehman and White
Galveston Bay / Sally E. Antrobus
Crossing the Rio Grande: An Immigrant's Life in the 1880s /
Gómez and Valdez
Birdlife of Houston, Galveston, and the Upper Texas Coast /
Eubanks and Behrstock
The Formation and Future of the Upper Texas Coast /
John B. Anderson
Finding Birds on the Great Texas Coastal Birding Trail /
Eubanks and Behrstock
Texas Coral Reefs / Cancelmo and Earle
Fishing Yesterday's Gulf Coast / Farley and McEachron
Fishes of the Texas Laguna Madre / McKee and Compton
The Louisiana Coast: Guide to an American Wetland /
Gay M. Gomez
Storm over the Bay: The People of Corpus Christi and Their Port /
Mary Jo O'Rear
After Ike: Aerial Views from the No-Fly Zone / Bryan Carlile
Kayaking the Texas Coast / John Whorff
Glory of the Silver King: The Golden Age of Tarpon Fishing /
Hart Stilwell, edited by Brandon Shuler
River Music: An Atchafalaya Story / Ann McCutchan
Del Pueblo: A History of Houston's Hispanic Community /
Thomas H. Kreneck